Broken
to
Broken

Urban Missions as a Path to Spiritual Growth

Jim Ellison

BROKEN TO BROKEN: Urban Missions as a Path to Spiritual Growth

ISBN 978-1-4951-3286-5

DEDICATION

To Beth, Will and Ben

The best place to be is together.

BROKEN TO BROKEN

TABLE OF CONTENTS

BROKEN TO BROKEN

FORWARD

Every authentic follower of Jesus Christ lives in the desire to be fruitful. Jim Ellison has delivered an inspiring personal testimony in *Broken to Broken* that will no doubt be an encouragement to many in their journey with Christ. In acknowledging his own brokenness and journey with those in need, Jim is able to create a starting point for many to move from a static place in their relationship with God to a fruit bearing life. In challenging us to "be with rather than just do for", we are moved to break through to a fruit bearing life and live in the ministry and mission of Christ to the least of these.

I commend this book that we not only own our brokenness, but that we also trust God to redeem that brokenness to his glory as we launch into a fruit bearing life to God's glory.

Steve Wood
Lead Pastor
Mount Pisgah United Methodist Church
Johns Creek, GA

BROKEN TO BROKEN

UNDERSTANDING THE "WHY" BEFORE BEGINNING

*"I came that they may have life and
have it to the full." John 10:10*

Growth is normal. Well, growth is normal for healthy,
living things—and there lies the tension in this book. In
life, it is feasible to breathe and sometimes not be fully
living, or at least not experience what Jesus referred to as
the abundant life (John 10:10). We have all experienced
seasons in life when we felt we were not growing in our
relationship with God. We were just going through the
motions of church attendance, occasional prayers, and
attending small Bible study groups when we realized
something was missing. Experiencing a "dry season" is
not abnormal; however, a stagnant relationship with the
Almighty creates a real problem.

Throughout *Broken to Broken*, I will refer to one's
"spiritual life" or "spiritual journey." What I mean by
"spiritual" is one's relationship with God, and specifically,
in relationship with the person of Jesus Christ. *Broken
to Broken* is written for those who already claim to be
followers of Jesus. I am not attempting to defend the
Christian faith nor convert non-believers to Christianity.
My intent here is to assist those of us who already
claim Jesus Lord and Son of God, to strengthen our

understanding of what it means to be a follower of Jesus and to grow in that special relationship.

Growing up on a farm in Fayette County, Georgia taught me one of the basic laws in nature—health leads to growth. Healthy plants produce abundant harvests. As simple as it sounds, the quickest way to determine if a plant is healthy or not, is to evaluate the quantity and quality of the harvest. This is why evaluating spiritual health is critical for any follower of Jesus.

The fruit of one's life speaks volumes.

Most of us do not like to evaluate ourselves spiritually. We do not want to take an honest inventory of how we have grown in our faith journeys and how God is currently using our lives for the Kingdom. The failure to self-examine leaves us missing out on the abundant life Jesus promised.

The conditioning of the soul naturally affects how we experience the Kingdom. Human sin, whether we know it or not, affects the progress of our faith journeys. Our brokenness, as a result of sin, impacts our spiritual growth more than most of us would admit. The probable cause of a barren life is our refusal to allow our brokenness and sin to be redeemed by God for God's purposes. The Kingdom life that Jesus offers cannot be fully realized unless everything in our lives (past as well as present), good and bad, is made available for redemption. By that, I mean putting it all upon the table of the Lord to be used for his ultimate purpose.

To experience fully the Kingdom is to live under God's governance. The Apostle Paul articulated Kingdom living when he described the "fruit of the Spirit" in his letter to the Galatians: love, joy, peace, patience, kindness, goodness, faithfulness, gentleness, and self-control

(Galatians 5:22-23). Kingdom living is living under the authority of God and continuing to make choices in our lives that honor Him. Living in God's Kingdom produces spiritual growth and a Christ-like life; however, choosing not to live in the Kingdom leads to spiritual decline in our lives and barrenness. This is the season of life in which too many followers of Jesus find themselves.

Spiritual drought, for many of us, has become the norm. Like many, I have stumbled along the spiritual valleys. Maneuvering through these valleys is like wading through a spiritual wasteland or desert. Although God is very much present throughout the valley, we fail to hear when the Almighty speaks. This unproductive life is hardly fulfilling because it is laced with frustration, hopelessness, and spiritual fatigue.

So if you are in a spiritual desert in your life, seeking restoration, wholeness, and healing, I am glad you have picked up this book. My genuine prayer is for you to gain a few new insights, rekindle your spiritual journey and move toward the life our God desires for you in his Kingdom.

Broken to Broken takes a non-traditional approach to spiritual growth and moving through one's spiritual desert. Many think spiritual growth only comes through study of scripture or by listening to sermons; the premise of my book is that the "broken to broken" relationships in our lives can become a catalyst for spiritual growth.

What I have discovered in my own brokenness is that we experience God's healing often by serving marginalized persons, the most vulnerable in society, in their poverty and brokenness. When we as broken and wounded Christians engage the marginalized with authenticity, just being with other broken persons can be a sure path for mutual growth, spiritual fulfillment, and genuine healing for all parties.

I have witnessed the power of God's healing as he uses persons in the inner city to help bring healing, redemption, and wholeness to those of us in the suburbs. Trust me, I have experienced brokenness and likewise, I have experienced healing. I have seen God use broken persons to help heal the broken. Specifically, I have seen God use urban missions as a catalyst to address our need for restoration and healing. God heals in the midst of "broken to broken" relationships.

God's grace is revealed when those of us who are broken and wounded seek to be with those who are also broken and wounded.

This book represents what I have learned through my own brokenness, and how God has used each season in my life to create a path for spiritual growth. While I do not have all the answers, I have seen God use my imperfections for His Kingdom's sake. I have seen brokenness redeemed for spiritual growth and restoration.

While brokenness is our reality in this world, restoration is God's promise and our hope.

Jim Ellison
March 22, 2014

Chapter 1

WIDE DOOR

"A wide door for effective work has opened to me."
I Corinthians 16:9

"I'm miserable. Something has got to change. Ministry is not supposed to be like this." I wrote these words in my journal as I sipped on my third cup of coffee after wondering throughout the night where things had gone wrong. I could not put my finger on it, but I knew in my heart and soul something was not right. Surely God had something more in store for me. What I did not know was that God was using my state of misery as a catalyst for spiritual growth. I knew God was not in the business of randomly punishing and creating despair for His children, however, my prayer was "God, what do I make of my misery?"

Being miserable has always been a precursor to God doing something new in my life. As I reflect upon my most dismal seasons, God has always been in the midst of my transitions, helping to change my environment, or more importantly, helping to change my heart and soul. You would not think a pastor would spend much time struggling with his spirituality, but I have dealt with a lack of fulfillment in ministry although by all appearances, I had it all together.

For almost two decades I enjoyed suburban ministry where strong children and student ministries, coupled with above average Sunday morning experiences, left worshippers saying, "Wow, we will be back!" Ministry in the suburbs was fun and exciting, but also safe and predictable. I grew accustomed to annual church growth, yet I knew deep within that something was missing. I was empty, struggling spiritually, and just going through the motions. Something had to change for me to experience fulfillment once again in ministry.

As I reflect upon that season of discomfort, I now see a lack of spiritual fulfillment. The abundant life promised by Jesus was far from reality in my life, but God was at work stirring up my soul. Although I did not know it, God was leading me and challenging me to a new door of opportunity in his Kingdom work. I felt he was leading me toward something new and very different in my life. In hindsight, I felt God was providing a needed holy nudge to force me from the comfort and security I was enjoying as a young, "successful" suburban pastor. All I had to do was discover what was behind that door God seemed to be opening for my life.

*Being miserable is a good sign God
wants to open a new door in your life.*

I know you have experienced similar seasons in your life. You cannot really put your finger on the "why," but you know in your heart a change is needed. You need a change at work, a change within your family, or most likely, a change deep within. It seems like we do a good job pointing out changes needed around us, while failing at the same time to acknowledge changes needed within ourselves. Usually, we want to reform or correct everything else, but self.

My faith journey has taught me God uses my misery and my own lack of satisfaction to reveal new opportunities that He wants me to experience in His Kingdom. Misery, as I have said, is a precursor to God doing new things in our lives.

Paul's words to the Corinthians hang on the door of my soul, "I will stay on at Ephesus until Pentecost, because a wide door for effective work has opened to me" (I Corinthians 16:8-9). Paul must have had an inward holy nudge prompting him to stay in Ephesus. Perhaps there was something more to be done for Christ. I believe Paul could see God opening doors for the sake of the Kingdom and the spreading of the faith. God was opening wider and broader doors leading to greater missionary work.

When it comes to serving in Christ's Kingdom, effective church work is very different from busy work. In today's culture, we have been trained to stay busy, which gets easier every day with ever more sophisticated cellphones, tablets, the Internet, and other high tech gadgets. Those of us who work in the church are especially good at "busy work." More programs, more meetings, and more reports have become our badge of honor! If you have grown accustomed to staying busy in church life as a volunteer or a staff person, the "good news" is that many will affirm you for your commitment to your religious organization. The "bad news" is seldom does busy church work lead to effectiveness in Christ's Kingdom and fulfillment of life he offers.

Entering the Open Door

As a pastor in the United Methodist Church, I was and am still under the spiritual authority of our bishop. Methodist pastors take a vow "to go where they are sent." So there was not much discussion when I received the phone call from my bishop: "You are going to downtown Atlanta to be the next pastor of the historic Atlanta First United Methodist Church on Peachtree Street." A wide door was opening.

Leaving the suburbs where I had helped plant a church, and where I saw God doing amazing work during my twelve years as senior pastor, was more difficult than I ever imagined. I was not completely sure I wanted to leave. To be honest, I struggled with fear of leaving the safety and comfort of suburban ministry. My family and I were leaving a hundred plus acre campus in the heart of one of the fastest growing counties in Metro Atlanta with multiple facilities and an extremely talented staff. Try to imagine leaving all that for one block of real estate at 360 Peachtree Street in downtown Atlanta, Georgia.

Despite being a declining congregation for previous decades, it was easy to see the opportunity for God's work at Atlanta First. I realized quickly that God wanted to do a much-needed new work within, and through, me in my new assignment. The limitations of my spiritual life, including a bunch of personal insecurities, had led me into a season where something drastically had to change. However, it was not exactly in a way that I may have anticipated.

Most of the time, God opens doors in his Kingdom which we could never have anticipated in our wildest dreams.

In the midst of this new urban ministry, I discovered God's healing power within my own brokenness. When you are serving in downtown Atlanta, you are surrounded with visible signs of brokenness. There are crumbling buildings, torn up streets, neglected infrastructure, shattered lives, and hoards of lost people with no place to call home but the streets. While spiritual brokenness is rampant in the suburbs, many of us who live outside the city try to conceal and camouflage pain. You do understand how it works, don't you? The more material possessions one accumulates, the easier it is to hide emptiness and dysfunction. Most of us have lived that life.

I have consistently found the marginalized on the streets to be very transparent. They do not possess symbols of success to cover up their pain, disorientation, or personality disorders. Truly, "what you see is what you get." I never thought I would say it, but time spent with the wounded, the broken, and the destitute, in the city was enlightening and somewhat satisfying. Authenticity can be beautiful. What I learned by serving those in the margins of society, those who are transparent with their own brokenness, is that I, too, have a deep sense of brokenness. I too am in need of constant mending and restoration.

By admitting my own brokenness I was drawn closer to those broken and with tormented souls within my reach. This led to an awareness of my own needs, healing, and redemption. Being with persons who openly admitted their personal struggles gave me permission to acknowledge my own plight, which led to spiritual growth and the restoration of my soul.

One of the benefits of working with the broken is that you come face to face with your own brokenness.

Control

Several years ago when my family purchased a new entertainment system for our home, I called a friend who installs such systems for his advice. Within a week, he and his team were in our home installing what I referred to as "the mother of all entertainment systems." Of course, it was not that spectacular compared to what is out there today, but it was unlike anything our family had ever owned. Where I grew up, "high tech" was a TV with a rabbit-ear-antenna wrapped in aluminum foil!

My friend began instructions by handing me a mechanical device saying, "Jim, this is your remote control, and you will learn to love it." Now understand, this was not your average remote control. It had more buttons and more options than I had ever seen on a remote, yet it fit perfectly in the palm of my hand. I was amazed at the functions I could control with that gadget. That afternoon, I quickly surpassed the novice level and was adjusting everything: discovering music channels, arranging sound throughout our home and surfing cable channels with ease. Life was good!

About a week after the new system was installed, Beth, my wife, nonchalantly commented, "I think you are enjoying that remote a little too much. Just don't get used to controlling everything!" Her words spoke truth deep within my soul and brought to the surface a part of my innermost being that is not very attractive to me. I really do not like to admit it publicly, but I like to be in control. I want to call the shots and I do most of the time. I also think that deep down inside, most of us, would admit enjoying some level of control in our lives. None of us easily relinquishes control to others, or submits easily to the power of others.

The problem we face as we seek to control our circumstances is we overlook doors of opportunities in Christ's Kingdom.

While taking responsibility for our actions, and being proactive, all of which is important in our spiritual journeys, we place ourselves in a spiritual jeopardy when we are obsessed with our wants and needs. Having the ability to attain all of our desires is dangerous. This level of power leads ultimately to the destruction of others and self. Most importantly, attempting to control every aspect of life blinds us from the Kingdom life God desires for us. Focusing upon the wrong door is much easier than discovering the wider door of opportunity God has in store for us.

Think back to the testimony of Paul. When discovering the new door of opportunity that God had opened for him (I Corinthians 16:8-9), his focus became honoring God with his life and also being a catalyst for Christ's Kingdom. Nowhere in this text was Paul concerned primarily about his own personal security or was he looking for ways to control what might happen to him next. Using his life for Christ's sake appeared to be Paul's only motive.

I am convinced it is God's will to open our hearts, so that we may see and experience new doors of opportunity in his Kingdom. These wide doors will lead us to a new and fruitful season of Kingdom work. The challenge we face,

I think, is not allowing our personal need for control to hinder us from seeing and experiencing this opportunity.

When I relinquished my desire for traditional church-based ministry, God revealed to me a new door of opportunity to serve Christ in urban missions. God has shown me during this season of ministry how I may experience healing myself while also helping to mend and heal others. I wonder how my life would have been different if I had continued to live with a self-centered focus that overshadowed God's Kingdom? When I gave up control of my life and prayed, "God, I desire to honor you with my life. How can I be the husband you have called me to be? The father? The pastor?" That prayer totally changed my life.

Reflection Questions

1. Regarding your spiritual life, how would currently grade yourself? What grade (A, B, C) fits your current spiritual state?

2. What do you think is the biggest hindrance you face in your spiritual journey?

3. Jim describes a time when he felt God opening a Kingdom door for him. Have you ever felt God doing the same for you? Did you walk through the Kingdom door and embrace the opportunity? Describe the experience.

4. Desiring to be in control is normal behavior. We like to call the shots in life. How can our need for control interfere with the life God wants for us in his Kingdom? Has your desire to control ever hindered a Kingdom opportunity in your life? What was the outcome?

5. What is one thing you might do this week to help you along your own spiritual journey?

BROKEN TO BROKEN

Chapter 2

THE OBVIOUS

"When he came to his senses..." Luke 15:17

Several years ago a friend invited me to go deep-sea fishing. Though I am far more experienced with fresh water fishing, I knew I would enjoy the time away with my buddy so I gladly accepted the invitation. There were four of us on the trip, including a professional guide who would "put us on the fish." The morning began with catching baitfish to be used later to catch our supper: grouper, snapper and amberjack. I was very excited, of course, and ready to catch something. Actually, I was ready to catch anything!

As soon as we anchored where we would catch bait, the guide handed me a five-gallon bucket and said, "Fill this with water for the bait-fish." Not wanting to miss a minute of fishing, I hurriedly began looking for the hose that I had seen earlier so I could complete my task of filling the bucket with water. However, the hose was nowhere to be found, and time was running out as my friends began pulling in our bait. I began to panic! Out of pure frustration, and with a touch of personal embarrassment, I said to the guide, "I'm sorry, but I cannot find the hose. Where do I get the water?"

At that moment the world seemed to stop. There was complete silence, and all eyes were upon me. My fellow fishermen waited to see how the guide would respond to my failure to complete the simple task of filling a bucket with water.

The guide paused, stretching his arms wide toward the deep blue ocean, and said, "Pastor, this is called the Gulf of Mexico. It will supply all the water you need for the task!" Everyone enjoyed a little humor at my expense, and I was relieved finally to fill the bucket with seawater!

Sometimes the obvious is not so obvious to us. What others plainly see, we plainly miss. This happens quite often when we look at ourselves. Our colleagues, friends, and family can see something that we have completely missed.

Self-assessment is a hard task. Who wants to take an honest look within asking the question: "What needs to change about me?" Pointing out the failures and shortcomings of others is certainly easier and less threatening. Sadly, for some, acknowledging the failures of others is infinitely more satisfying, and can be addictive. Society conditions us to focus upon the flaws in others rather than making honest appraisal of ourselves.

A lack of self-assessment is toxic to the soul.

Guess what? You and I are not perfect. We all have our flaws, our shortcomings, and our secret sins. Becoming self-aware of this need for our soul's healing is the key to experiencing complete restoration. It is impossible to get well without acknowledging our need for the One who heals.

Restoration ATL

The ministry I currently lead, Restoration ATL (RATL), helps women and children transition out of homelessness. Groups from across the southeast come to downtown Atlanta to take part in weekend spiritual retreats with homeless families through RATL. Far more than an inner-city mission project, RATL creates an environment where the obvious is made even more obvious.

You see, most of the groups coming into the city to serve do so with the best intentions. They come to help those who are obviously in need. Each weekend, volunteers arrive excited and ready to take part in the restoration process of women and children living in Atlanta's largest shelter. What actually happens, however, is that these groups come face-to-face with their own need for restoration. Men and women, young and old, who have chosen to give a weekend of their lives to serve the poor, quickly realize God has them on the weekend retreat to make them aware of the obvious. Each of us is broken, and in need of restorative healing.

During a reflection time not long after we started RATL, one of the volunteers confessed to the group, "I came this weekend expecting to help a homeless person, but what I've discovered, is that I needed this trip far more than I realized. I came to offer a little help, but in all reality, I'm the one who needed the help." Nods of affirmation followed her comment. The circled group of volunteers agreed God was in the process of revealing to them their own spiritual need. In the midst of the broken, the homeless, and those who are in obvious need of restoration, God reveals the universal need for restoration and wholeness.

When you are immersed in a culture of brokenness, you become aware of your own need for restoration. The obvious becomes obvious.

Healing begins with the acknowledgement of our brokenness.

Do you remember how the prodigal son (Luke 15) responded when he found himself in a foreign country, hungry, and desiring to eat with the pigs (15:16)? Desperate times will indeed lead to desperation. Surrounded by everything he despised, coupled with shame and regret, Luke describes perfectly the moment when what is obvious becomes very clear to the wayward soul:

"When he came to his senses..." Luke 15:17

Though it sounds counter-intuitive, the blessing the prodigal experienced prior to coming to his senses is that he realized he had lost everything. He was a loser. Of course, we know that he still had his father's love and acceptance, but the prodigal had lost what was important to him—his self-identity. Until he came to his senses, he had forgotten that he belonged to his father. He had forgotten that he needed his father. He had forgotten that trying to live without his father would lead to emptiness and ultimately destruction. Before coming to his senses, the prodigal was living in a state of denial. Sadly, it took finding himself in a place of deep brokenness before he acknowledged the obvious. He needed a healthy relationship with his father.

Experiencing loss can become a catalyst to our coming to our senses.

I believe when we realize there is a dimension in our life that is broken and in need of immediate attention, it is a special gift from God. How many people do you know who changed their daily habits only after discovering something was seriously wrong with them? The person, who has a heart attack and immediately starts to eat better and exercise, will tell you fear is a great motivator. The student needing to finish her high school career with a 3.0 GPA in order to receive a scholarship who enters her senior year with a 2.8 GPA becomes very serious with her study habits. The worker who has been reprimanded for tardiness to work and is in danger of losing his job with another tardy, finds the energy to get up earlier in order to arrive on time.

The fear of losing something important is not only threatening, but it can persuade one to make drastic changes! Think back to a time when you were in danger of losing something important to you. Perhaps it was a job, a scholarship, a child, a marriage, or perhaps your soul. The fear of loss can be a wonderful thing. Looking back on my life, when I was in danger of losing something dear to me, the impetus for change was easy. Being on the verge of losing what is important can be a real blessing in disguise. As we acknowledge and implement the necessary changes in our lives, God honors healthy change by providing us with peace of mind and rest for our souls.

Realizing changes need to be made
leads to freedom and peace.

I have paid the high price for attempting to live without addressing my broken soul. I have learned that before I can experience wholeness and healing myself, I must first, "come to my senses" and acknowledge the obvious: I am broken and I cannot fix myself. Becoming aware of self is a beautiful gift from God, yet sadly, many of us go through life without introspection or assessment.

One of the dangers of finding security in material possessions is that our abundance of resources serves to cover up the poverty and brokenness of our souls. I have seen this covering up process over and over, followed by the inevitable crash. I have seen this old broken story played out in marriages, parent-child relationships, business partnerships, ministries, and the list goes on and on. To go through one's life camouflaging brokenness is taxing to the soul, suffocates our spiritual life, and if not addressed, will lead to an emotional train wreck, burnout, or nervous breakdown.

Ronnie was a successful businessman, married father of three children, and living his dream in a "McMansion" in one of Atlanta's elite communities. Life appeared good for Ronnie, but he knew something was missing. Somewhere behind the scenes, Ronnie's marriage was mundane at best. His children were busy in sports and Ronnie's wife drove the family taxi seven days a week. However, Ronnie began to question how well he even knew his kids. While the money was good, Ronnie wondered if what he was doing at work really made a difference at all, and more importantly, he questioned the influence he was having as a husband and father of three teenagers.

From all appearances, Ronnie was living the good life. He even had a bumper sticker with "Life is Good!" displayed on his SUV telling the world that he was doing just fine, but it was just a cover-up. Ronnie knew what so many have come to experience in the midst of the "good life." Ronnie was discovering that the more material stuff we possess, the easier it is to cover up our pains, fears, and insecurities.

Ronnie and I connected while I was pastoring in downtown Atlanta. Shortly after he and his family started attending church, Ronnie found himself getting involved in local missions, reaching out to the homeless, and serving the poor. Within months, Ronnie was taking off layers of his upscale veneer. As Ronnie served alongside the vulnerable, I saw restoration in the lives of those in the street, but also in the life of Ronnie. Being with the poor, the broken, the destitute, and homeless provided Ronnie the opportunity to claim his own brokenness, needs, and dysfunctions. Ronnie told me,

> *"I've paid thousands of dollars to counselors over the years. I could have saved a lot of money by serving the poor instead."*

What they really need is Jesus

One of the spiritual dangers to those with financial resources is believing there is some correlation between having money and being spiritually mature and happy. I faced this in the suburbs more than one would imagine. Having a large roof over your head does not equate to being spiritually sound or having it all together.

I met Jay while speaking to a group of church members after a Wednesday night dinner. We had been discussing homelessness, poverty, and some of the challenges the poor face on a daily basis. Our time was coming to a close when Jay said, "What they really need is Jesus."

I took a moment to reflect on my new friend's well-intended comment. He was correct; the poor do need Jesus. We all need Jesus. Right? But there was something missing in his words. I could not help but worry that Jay had missed the point I was trying to communicate that evening. It was the point that many of us are in danger of missing all together.

Poverty is universal. Not everyone experiences material poverty, but everyone experiences some form of poverty, whether it is emotional, physical, or spiritual. Without immersing ourselves in a culture of brokenness, it is easy to overlook our own level of brokenness. Living in our cocoon or "bubble" has a way of blinding us to our need for the restoration and healing of our souls.

Immersing ourselves in brokenness
makes us aware of our poverty.

My Facebook Life

I have been learning to use Facebook. I did not jump into social media right away, but in recent years, I have joined a billion of my closest friends, and am now an avid user of the communication phenomenon. I confess that I am still trying to understand the purpose of Twitter, Vine, Snapchat and Instagram. However, I do understand the purpose of Facebook, and the rules for effective posting.

For example, one of the first lessons is to post only comments and pictures that make you look like you are living the "good life." Happy and stylish are always better options than struggling, disheveled, and down-on-your-luck. I know you would not do it, but some people delete pictures of themselves because the photo is not flattering enough for Facebook. Most of us look for cool dated photos to post on TBT (that's "Throw back Thursdays" for you social media novices) to remind our friends of who we were before the day of Facebook, back during a skinnier season of life.

What you do not see on Facebook is recognition of brokenness, human need, and emptiness. Do you know anyone who posts their deepest fears, doubts, and struggles on Facebook? When was the last time you saw someone post anything that hinted at a need for healing? Have you ever heard of someone confessing that she needed help spiritually? Such posts seldom make it on Facebook. Most Facebook postings give the appearance that all is well, very good, and better-than-average in the author's almost perfect life. Is it any wonder why more than a billion people have signed up for Facebook?

The Human Condition

Brokenness is the inescapable human condition. The need for restoration and healing is universal; if we do not acknowledge our depravity, we will live our lives pretty much with tormented souls. Our only option, it seems to me, is to face it, and seek healing and wholeness. The good news is that dealing with our brokenness leads to freedom and peace. We will discuss in the chapters ahead how God uses the marginalized to help us experience the spiritual restoration of our souls. We will see, not only that restoration is possible, but also the life God has in store for us on the other side of our brokenness, is a life of fulfillment.

Let the restoration begin.

Reflection Questions

1. When did you come close to losing something important to you? How did you change your behavior to keep what you had? How long did it take before you "came to your senses" like the prodigal son?
2. Most of us are not very self-aware. What keeps us from being honest with ourselves and with others regarding our brokenness?
3. Obviously, each of us fosters our own level of brokenness. When was a time you became aware of your need for healing? How did you discover something needed changing in your life?
4. When you hear the word, "restoration," what comes to mind? What is the role of "restoration" in our faith journey?
5. What are some practical steps you could implement in your life that would lead to self-awareness and a journey towards restoring your soul?

Chapter 3

TRANSPARENCY

"Do you want to get well?" John 5:6

Richard fought the demon of crack cocaine for well over a decade. When I met him he had lost everything he considered important in life: his family, his health, his work and, most importantly, knowledge that he was a child of God and that spiritual restoration was an option.

I met Richard when he began attending a new Sunday evening worship service at Atlanta First United Methodist Church created to connect with people on the streets and in the shelters in Atlanta. While the service quickly started reaching young people in the city and families from the suburbs, connecting with people like Richard was the original catalyst for launching it. Within a month of starting the service, Richard, who was nearing graduation from his substance abuse rehabilitation program, entered the historic sanctuary on Peachtree Street.

It did not take Richard long to begin serving. He volunteered to lead a Bible study of substance abusers, some former and some active. Richard brought many of his friends to the Bible study and evening service. He was a strong leader in the church, present every week, until he suddenly vanished. When I say, "vanished," I mean that he literally disappeared over night. He was nowhere to be found. I was unable to reach him through his rehabilitation program. Within weeks, his phone had been disconnected. I feared the demon of crack cocaine had surfaced once again in his life.

Six months passed without a word from Richard. Then out of the blue, he called. "Pastor Jim, this is Richard. Can I come and see you?" Within a few hours, I sat face to face with Richard while he shared what had happened to him. "One beer led to two beers, which ultimately led to getting back on the pipe. I found myself entangled once again in the devil's web." As he opened his broken heart to me, repenting of his actions, he said: "The temptation is one I face each day. I'm reminded daily of my weakness. I just question if healing is possible."

Richard's words pierced my soul. The reality for each of us is that Richard's story is our story; we just suffer from different addictions and temptations. As Richard struggled with how to overcome his brokenness, I could not help but question my own brokenness and wonder how one moves forward as a cracked vessel or broken jar? Is spiritual restoration possible? Can God redeem our brokenness? With the baggage we have created, is spiritual healing a real possibility? Can God use our pasts with our good, bad, and ugly moments, for the Kingdom's sake? Richard's vulnerability taught me that admitting brokenness to others begins the long process for healing.

We really do not like to talk about our own brokenness. We do not like to admit that all is not good with our souls. I particularly like how Gordon Cosby, co-founder and pastor of the Church of the Savior in Washington, DC, describes our personal brokenness. He says, "Every person you meet sits beside his or her own pool of tears." Brokenness is indeed the universal dilemma.

Admitting brokenness is not something we naturally do. Reading that you are sitting by a pool of your own tears may make you uneasy since we do not like to admit we do not have it together. The question we must face is: How do we move forward in the midst of our brokenness? Is restoration possible? As my friend, Ed Nelson asks, "Can Humpty Dumpty be put together again?" Maybe before asking if healing is an option, we need to honestly ask ourselves if we truly desire healing.

Seeking Wholeness

Do you remember the story in John 5 of the man sitting by the pool where the physically impaired and broken gathered to be healed? They believed when the water in the pool was stirred, the first to get in would be healed. John describes the scene as a place where, "a great number of disabled people used to lie" (5:3) in hopes of a Divine touch.

According to John, Jesus made his way through the crowded area and saw this man who was waiting for the chance to be healed. John says the man had been waiting to be healed for thirty-eight years (John 5:5). During Jesus' day, that was nearly an entire lifetime. Can you imagine hanging out in any place that long?

Picture the scene: a bunch of crippled and lame people lying around the pool of water, desperately hoping to be healed while Jesus makes his way through the crowd. He discovers this man who has waited for thirty-eight years and poses the question, "Do you want to get well?" (John 5:6).

Really? What kind of question is that for a man who has lain, crippled and waiting by the pool thirty-eight years? Why would Jesus ask such a question? Jesus could have been implying that maybe some who are broken are not interested in experiencing healing. Can it be possible that not all broken people truly want to be made well? When we offer excuses for our condition, we often reveal our lack of desire for change. Read the rest of John 5 to see a litany of excuses the lame man gives. While it is hard to imagine, not all people who are spiritually and emotionally impaired, lame, or sick, really want to be healed.

A deep desire for healing must be chosen.

Although each of us deals with our own level of brokenness, seeking to be healed is a choice. I know when something needs changing in my own life. I know when a part of my soul is broken and needs repairing. However, I do not always take action. It is often easier to wallow in our misery than it is to be proactive, seek help, and make changes that will bring a sense of peace. Perhaps Jesus' question is appropriate for you today. "Do you want to get well?"

Vulnerability

Very few of us will get well by sitting still, by just waiting around for God to do something without our participation. Healing takes some desire on our part. Nothing enables healing quicker than our seeking help for our brokenness, often from those who appear most unlikely to help us. Healing comes when we admit we are broken and commit to pursuing restoration.

God uses our vulnerability to strengthen us. How can that be? It is one of those paradoxical mysteries of our faith. When Paul was struggling with his "thorn in the flesh" Jesus' response is a reminder that our admitting weakness is a catalyst for God's assistance. God said, "My grace is sufficient for you, for my power is made perfect in weakness" (2 Corinthians 12:9). When we admit we are weak, God intervenes and provides help. In my experience as a pastor, I have seen God provide healing for many broken souls but I have never seen God intervene and heal where He was not wanted.

God honors vulnerability by offering restoration.

When we confess that we are broken and in need of healing, God grants us whatever we need. We are not likely to experience God's healing touch without first acknowledging our own brokenness. Admitting brokenness is not easy. As a matter of fact, the more we appear to have our life intact, the more difficult it is to say, "Lord, help me! I am weighed down by my burdens and hurts."

In my spiritual journey, God revealed his grace to me when I admitted my brokenness and sought healing among others who also accepted their brokenness. God does indeed honor our vulnerability.

Alcoholics Anonymous

I had always heard about AA meetings and, as a pastor, I encouraged individuals to find a meeting they could attend. I even had my own copy of the AA "Big Book," but had never attended a meeting.

When my friend Robert (not his real name) invited me to attend an AA meeting with him, I agreed so I could experience this, therapeutic, worldwide movement that has help save so many lives from further destruction and disaster. I wanted a better understanding of why so many people were drawn to these one-hour sessions, led not by professional counselors, but by fellow recovering alcoholics.

"My name is John, and I'm an alcoholic." "My name is Shelley, and I'm an alcoholic." I did not know quite what to say when it was time to introduce myself.

Robert introduced me as his pastor and I said, "Hello, my name is Jim. I'm an addict. I don't fight the demon of alcohol but I sure have many other demons." Immediately, I was welcomed as a fellow traveler in need. No one flinched or looked at me like I had leprosy. Clearly, I had shattered no preconceived pastoral stereotypes!

The biggest hurdle for me was realizing that everyone was so accepting within the AA circle. There was a beautiful expression of unconditional acceptance coupled with personal accountability. I felt God's presence in a powerful way and I could see God using the broken to heal the brokenness inside my life.

Vulnerability is the foundation for experiencing wholeness and healing.

While members of AA have experienced the power of vulnerability for decades, career success can hinder one from being vulnerable, or admitting we are broken. Looking back upon my life during those most painful seasons, the only thing I was halfway successful at doing was hiding and trying to cover up my brokenness.

Success has a way of deadening our pain. Like taking a shot of Novocain, our "wins and victories" have a way of numbing us from pain we might otherwise be experiencing. I see it all the time in "successful men." Often when their job is good, the money is good, and the trips are good, that "successful man's" family is falling apart and going to hell in a handbasket. So often our "good life" covers up our "real life."

I credit my journey toward wholeness to God's use of other broken people to help me in my own healing. Even today, God seems to lead me to spend time examining my brokenness and being vulnerable with other broken people. This is how God continues to restore my life. Through the brokenness of others, I have been able to embrace my brokenness and seek restoration.

Broken to broken is the successful formula God uses for restoration.

Holy Nudge

"How have you heard God speaking to you tonight?" I ask that question many times in debriefing meetings during our spiritual retreats at the homeless shelter. Not everyone experiences what I call "the Holy Nudge," on the first night of the retreat, but sometimes, our spirits are ready to listen and the Voice is clear.

The responses usually go like this: "I am amazed at how much joy the residents seem to have. God helped me know that I need more joy in my life." "The residents here at the shelter are so accepting of me. I need to be more accepting of others." This particular night was different; I could sense the Holy Spirit working at a deeper level in the circle of suburbanites who had given a weekend of their lives to spend with homeless women and children.

"I've been clean for seven years," is not what you expect to hear from a mom who has brought her family to the inner city to serve the marginalized. Husbands, wives, elementary age children and teenagers sat in the circle where silence filled the room. While my first instinct was to speak, I listened for her next words.

"I've fought addiction for years. I came close to losing everything, but by God's grace, I will have been clean for seven years next month. Tonight, I met a resident who has also struggled with addiction for years. I encouraged her, and she encouraged me. God allowed our paths to cross tonight so we could help each other. Meeting her was like a divine appointment."

Divine Appointments

Admitting vulnerability and being transparent, lead to divine appointments. Denying our own brokenness may impede God's work in our lives, delaying our healing. If we really want to be well, vulnerability will help us find our path to healing.

We usually find that which we seek. My parents used to tell me, "If you look for trouble you will find it!" It is so true. Usually we find what it is we are looking for: the good or bad, the Kingdom life or worldly pathways that lead us away from Kingdom living.

Our days are filled with God appointments—
some we make, some we don't.

I do not believe in chance Kingdom experiences. God orchestrates these divine appointments throughout our days so we can experience restoration and build a little of his Kingdom within and around us. God can use every circumstance to bring healing in our lives and to strengthen His people. While I am amazed at the times God has placed in my path exactly the right person to encourage me, or a person who needed a word of encouragement from me, I cannot help but wonder how many appointments I did not recognize.

Alignment

I am not very mechanical when it comes to cars but I am pretty good at knowing when the oil needs changing. Regarding the mechanics of a vehicle, I do not have a clue. As long as the ride is smooth, I have no worries! Lucky for me, Jeff, my mechanic, helps me keep my vehicle in good shape.

Recently while getting my oil changed, Jeff told me my truck needed a front alignment. He showed me wear and tear on my tires and said, "Alignments affect a vehicle's performance. Unless your alignment is fixed, your truck will not drive properly. One tire out of alignment can greatly impact the performance of your truck."

I immediately thought, "Now that could preach!" Alignment affects performance. The people who recognize their divine appointments are engaged daily in intentional spiritual habits. They are practicing their faith by aligning themselves with God's will and allowing scripture, prayer, and holy conversations to shape them. Being vulnerable, acknowledging our periodic need for correct alignment with God, will increase our chances of realizing our divine appointments.

Broken Appointments

Every person we encounter carries burdens and hurts, and has spent some time in the valley of regret. When I share my angst, inner demons, and personal struggles with my counselor, I find comfort in knowing he, too, has his struggles. My admiration for Kingdom laborers like Mother Teresa and Billy Graham has less to do with their particular gifts and accomplishments, and more to do with their humble servitude. I am inspired by their daily struggle to love more deeply and fully. Real saints do not pretend; they acknowledge their brokenness and marvel at God's grace in their lives. They seek to offer that grace to other broken people. Vulnerability begets vulnerability in all of us. Lowering our self-protecting walls, being transparent, really is a beautiful thing!

Reflection Questions

1. Can you identify a time when you shared with a friend or counselor a personal burden or an aspect of brokenness that you carried in your life? How did the conversation affect you?

2. Why are we so timid in exposing our brokenness to others? What are the negative consequences of being vulnerable? What are the rewards?

3. The crippled man beside the pool (John 5) was certainly aware of his need for restoration, but Jesus' question causes us to wonder if the man really desired healing. Why do some refuse to transition from acknowledging their brokenness to doing something about it? What are the consequences of not being proactive in finding personal restoration?

4. We say "God uses the broken people to help heal broken people." Can you identify a time God used vulnerable people to enable you to look at your own life? What about a time when God used your brokenness to help another?

5. Do you have anyone in your life with whom you can be transparent? What steps do you take to share your vulnerability with others?

BROKEN TO BROKEN

Chapter 4

BE WITH

"He has sent me..." Luke 4:18

A friend of mine created a saying that describes how many experience inner city missions: "Ghetto Tourism." Drive in, drop off, take a peep, and drive back to the suburbs. This model of urban ministry represents more than 90 percent of ministry I witness in downtown Atlanta. Serving the marginalized in the city has taught me that many see urban ministry much like window-shopping. It is okay to get close enough to look casually, but nothing more. Do not get too close. If you have time, maybe taking a picture will do. Those taking the tour get a quick glimpse of another culture by observing the locals and feel pretty good when they leave. They seem pleased with themselves for having made the effort to do inner city ministry.

Seeing poverty up close can be educational, but "Ghetto Tourism" will not cut it. Observing the marginalized from a distance does not lead to restoration and it is not transformative. You may leave the ghetto with a feel-good sensation, but the reality is that no lives were changed. Checking your "mission box" and moving on with life does not lead to life-change. At best you will have a picture to post on Facebook.

One of the challenges of doing Kingdom work in the ghetto is that this type of ministry requires a significant investment of time rather than just money. In my twenty-five plus years being a pastor, I have taken groups of well-intentioned parishioners to "do mission work" in the city. This traditional model of urban ministry is based upon the transaction model: I will give you something you need (water bottle, food, clothing) and in exchange you express gratitude in order to meet my need for self-worth and accomplishment.

If you have done mission work in urban areas, there is a good chance you have practiced this model of "traditional urban missions." There are corners in downtown Atlanta where you can literally park your vehicle and toss sandwiches to homeless men and women, without ever speaking to them. Ghetto Tourism is quick, sanitized, and often self-serving.

The underlying problem with "Ghetto Tourism" is that the tourists, or sightseers, do not spend any time relating to or connecting with the marginalized, and consequently, nothing changes for them or us. The entire mission experience is observing or giving away something to the poor. Tourists usually do not take the time to learn names, to listen, and to laugh with those excluded from society. Simply put, tourists are more apt to focus on DOING FOR rather than BEING WITH the marginalized.

"BEING WITH" is more transformative
than "DOING FOR."

Katie had been at the homeless shelter for about three weeks when she began attending our Saturday morning program. She became an active participant and appeared to enjoy her time with our weekend volunteers. Every time I heard her speak during devotion time, she was pleasant and calm until the topic of "Ghetto Tourism" came up one Saturday.

"Pastor Jim, you wouldn't believe some churches. There is this one church that used to show up on Sunday afternoons at the parking lot two blocks up from the Greyhound Bus Station. They parked their cars and started handing out brown bags with sandwiches and a piece of fruit without ever speaking to us. Last week I had to tell one of their members 'quit taking pictures of us.' I asked her if she thought she was at the Atlanta Zoo."

It pains me to share that story. Can you imagine how Katie must have felt when she saw that church bus appear? The last place she wanted to be was standing in line waiting for a brown sack of food to help her make it until her next meal. Katie wanted to be treated like a fellow human being, a child of God. Yes, she was hungry and needed food, but more importantly, she needed human relationships. Rather than someone doing something for her, she needed someone to choose to be in relationship with her.

Redefining Urban Missions

Each weekend throughout the year we have groups from all over the southeast in Atlanta to participate in a Restoration ATL retreat. We spend the orientation describing the concept of "being with" the poor and deprogramming most volunteers' innate desire to want to do something for the marginalized, like serving a meal or cleaning up afterwards.

Before orientation, the most frequent question is, "Jim, what are we going to be doing this weekend?" Most of us are comfortable with doing. It makes us feel as if we are making a real difference. However, the impact of our work for Christ's Kingdom is minimal if we stop at only "doing for" and miss the opportunity to "be with" others. In "doing for" others, it is possible to miss the Kingdom experience God desires for us.

This traditional model of inner-city mission, "doing for," is ingrained in us. When we build, clean, make, do or give something to those in need it does not require the investment of "being with" another person. The Kingdom result is far less in trying "to do" as well. Not much spiritual restoration takes place for the one who lives in the street or one who worships in the pew the next Sunday.

Restoration is a result of "being with" not "doing for."

Jesus on "Being With"

Jesus understood the power of "with." He understood the importance of being involved in the lives of others. Our Lord's life on earth followed a pattern we would be wise to emulate. People ask me all the time, "How did you come up with this new concept of urban missions?" Each time I hear that question I respond by saying, "It's an idea that has been around for over 2000 years."

Do you remember Luke's description of Jesus beginning his public ministry in his hometown, Nazareth (Luke 4:16-30)? You will see that folks in Jesus' hometown were not as keen on relating to the marginalized as Jesus was. His mission to reach out to gentiles and outsiders was not what those who had gathered in the synagogue were accustomed to hearing. Apparently, religious folks from

Jesus' hometown had not included the marginalized as part of their faith community.

"The Spirit of The Lord is upon me, because he has anointed me to bring good news to the poor. He has sent me to proclaim release to the captives and recovery of sight to the blind, to let the oppressed go free, to proclaim the year of the Lord's favor" (Luke 4:18-19).

The poor, the captives and the oppressed all shared one thing: they represented the underclass in their society. They were among the marginalized, the outcasts, the nobodies in the ancient world. They did not play a significant role in Jesus' culture and the same is true today. If any of these groups was to make the evening news, rest assured that it would not be "good news."

Jesus, however, introduced a new approach when he began his public ministry in Nazareth. When Jesus was given the scroll of the prophet Isaiah, he unrolled the text (Isaiah 61) and began reading. The message was radical. Essentially, Jesus was saying, "I am the anointed one who you have been waiting for whether you know it or not. I have come to be with the broken. I have come to be with the marginalized." Here I am paraphrasing Isaiah 61:1-2. Jesus' message was explicit. "If you want to be part of this new Kingdom, you'll find me, the Anointed One, the Messiah, among those who have to live on the boundaries of society." Jesus' message was not well received. His desire to "be with" outcasts eventually got him kicked out of town (Luke 4:29).

As we follow Jesus throughout his earthly ministry, he consistently focused on being with those who were broken. Jesus practiced "being with" those who were in need of healing. He made a point to be compassionate to those who were alone and suffering.

Intentionality

"Being with" requires intentionality. As I have observed the Kingdom play out in my own life, I have learned that if I am going to be with the underclass, then I have to be where they are and be there for them and with them. Connecting with the alienated does not just happen; much energy and spiritual resolve are required. Entering environments of estrangement provide opportunities for God to do a new work in your soul.

Pastor Bruce Deel is the founder and CEO of the City of Refuge, where we run Restoration ATL. Under Pastor Bruce's leadership, the City of Refuge has become Atlanta's largest shelter for homeless women and children. He speaks throughout the country, sharing his story of the City of Refuge and real life Kingdom impact upon real persons in our city. Needless to say, God has continued to bless Bruce's good work for Christ's Kingdom.

Recently I was in a meeting with Bruce and he shared a story that touched my heart and soul. He was flying home from a speaking engagement where he had shared the history of the City of Refuge and examples of persons whose lives had been changed because of the mission. As he was reflecting upon the message he had given, it dawned on him the stories he shared were from years back. He said, "I have stories from years ago. I need more yesterday stories. I need more current stories." He went on to share his vision with the leadership team at the City of Refuge. He challenged us to be intentional in "being with" the women and children on campus.

When you are with the homeless, you experience change deep within your own soul. I do not leave a conversation with a wounded, broken person without experiencing some healing myself. Many times after spending time with a broken soul, I have heard the Spirit whisper, "He restoreth my soul" (Psalms 23:3).

Broken people spending quality time with other broken, hurting people leads to restoration.

I am skeptical when I hear someone mention the "one thing" or the "secret sauce" that makes a business or program successful. I have read my fair share of books on business and I know there really is not a "one thing" that guarantees 100% success. But, when asked, "What has been the catalyst that makes Restoration ATL what it is today?" I talk about this mission model of "being with." There are other factors that contribute to our growth, but nothing is greater than our revised approach of participating in urban ministry. "Being with" the marginalized is what leads to transformation. Again and again, I hear testimonies from those whose lives have been altered because they chose to spend a weekend with women and children who are transitioning out of homelessness.

Learn With

It is essential that groups coming into the city for a RATL retreat not begin their weekend with the idea that they are on the retreat "to help" the residents at the shelter. While the volunteers do provide wonderful counsel and support for the women and children on campus, it does not take long before the volunteers realize the residents have much to teach each of us if we trust the process of the retreat.

"While I believe God has brought you here this weekend 'to help' the residents, I believe the residents are equally here 'to help' us just as much. They have as much to teach us as we have to teach them. Some of the residents have more to teach us than we have to teach them." While silence filled the room, I sat waiting for responses from the volunteers. I continued, "I have become aware that I am the student. I have learned more about perseverance, faithfulness, and hope through urban missions than I ever learned while doing graduate work in theology."

If I lost everything of value, I want to believe that my faith in Christ would not fail me. If I was unemployed, facing what appeared to be a hopeless situation, I want to believe I would remain hopeful for a new and exciting future God has prepared for me. The reality is: I have never lost everything of importance to me. I have never encountered a season of pure absolute despair. Although I have spent nights in a homeless shelter, staying was a choice. Odds are, you have never been to the point of sleeping in a homeless shelter. Imagine what you could learn from someone who is materially poor and spiritually rich.

We hear from God when we spend time with the broken.

I was Sheila's pastor in Atlanta. When we met, she was dressed in her native African attire and wearing a beautiful hat she had made for Sunday's worship service. She was animated and shared a passion for Christ, which was genuine because it came from her pure heart and soul.

A few days later, Sheila came by our church office where we had a lengthy conversation about faith. Within moments of hearing her story, I could sense this meeting of heart as a Divine appointment. After a month of regular conversations with her, I confess that I did not know whether Sheila had what I call a "double dose of the Holy Spirit" or if she struggled with some form of mental illness. Listening to her stories of faith inspired and encouraged me; they left me questioning if I was conversing with a child of God who was in touch with the Almighty in a different way than I had experienced. It was one of the most unique encounters of pastor/parishioner relationships I have been privileged to experience.

One Sunday morning prior to worship, Sheila cornered me and threw a wad of cash at me. After picking up a few stray bills in the sanctuary, I quickly started counting them. Sheila interrupted my counting and blurted out loud enough for the people on the other side of the sanctuary to hear, "Pastor Jim, why are you counting? There's no need to count that money because God told me to give it to you. Take all of it. It's $600."

I was shocked by her generous gift. Knowing she had an annual income of less than $3,500 and was living on food stamps in subsidized housing, I immediately questioned her, "Sheila, are you sure?"

"Of course I'm sure, Pastor Jim. God told me to give it to you. I am just being obedient. Give it to Elliott to pass on to Emily." Elliott was our staff pastor of missions. In preparing for a semester of mission work in Africa, Elliott's daughter, Emily, had sent letters to family and friends, requesting financial support for her mission experience.

Following the service, I gave the money to Elliott for Emily. I told Elliott how Sheila had thrown the money at me, and that it totaled $600. Elliott smiled as he listened and said, "Well, what you don't know is that after Emily received funding from her appeal, she was $590 short."

I could not believe what I was hearing. I said to Elliott, "See, God still speaks to people." Elliott replied. "I am not surprised God spoke to Sheila. I am surprised that there are still people who listen to God and who obey his voice."

Like so many who live in the periphery of society, Sheila taught me faithfulness and obedience in the midst of my own uncertainty. By spending time with Sheila and others who live in the city, I have seen what it means to "trust and obey" under dire circumstances. Those who live in poverty have taught me that my personal identity is not found in my pastoral role or the accumulation of material things, but in being a "child of God," a husband to Beth, and father to Will and Ben. Our real identity as Christians is ultimately found in Christ.

Worship and Bingo

You would not think worshipping with the underprivileged and playing Bingo with them would have much in common, but I learned otherwise. I noticed the popularity of both events soon after we started Restoration ATL.

From the beginning, weekend spiritual retreats included both activities, but I could not figure out why they were so popular. Why would women who were transitioning out of homelessness enjoy worship and playing Bingo with suburban women so much? Then it dawned on me: while everyone was worshipping God and playing Bingo, everyone was equally involved.

Think about the similarities. When the Bingo cards are passed out, everyone is in the same boat. No one has an advantage over anyone else. One card is equal to another card. Position, power, and possessions do not influence the outcome of the game. The female struggling just to read, dealing with self-esteem issues, or who recently completed her rehabilitation program, has the same chance of winning as the volunteer from the suburbs who is giving her weekend to serve on the RATL retreat.

When the same women spend time worshipping with each other, both are in need of God's mercy and grace. Whether one lives in a house or sleeps in bed at a shelter, whether one holds a graduate degree or has passed her GED, or drives an SUV or pushes a shopping cart down the street, when worshipping God everyone has equal footing and place.

Worshipping "With" Levels the Playing Field

When I worship with the poor, I come face to face with the reality that nothing, absolutely nothing, separates me spiritually from those with whom I share the pew. This is humbling considering I enjoy being the one who hands out water bottles in the summer and skull caps in the winter. When I am before God, worshipping Him, I am completely in need, just like everyone else, of Divine spiritual healing.

"Being With" Changes Perspective

As I reflect upon my faith journey and what it means to be with the poor, my perspective toward others has changed. I am constantly reminded of Stephen Covey's principle in his classic book, Seven Habits of Highly Effective People.

He writes that we must "Seek first to understand before seeking to be understood."

*"Being with" helps us understand a culture
very different from our own.*

William was not your typical, homeless person out on the street. He was homeless by choice, he was retired with a pension, and he owned and maintained a vehicle. He was always dressed nicely for worship and periodically he brought other homeless people with him.

While talking with William one Sunday before evening service, I asked him about his children. He responded: "Pastor Jim, I have three boys. The youngest is doing great. He is married, lives on the south side of Atlanta, and has two children. My middle son is in heaven. He was murdered when he was twenty-two. And my oldest son, he is doing life. He killed a man about ten years ago."

I honestly did not know how to respond to William. He was so matter-of-fact and honest. I stood there stunned at the idea of having both a murdered son and a son who was a murderer. I said, "William, I am so sorry to hear about your two oldest sons. I can not even imagine how painful their stories must be for you." He nodded and said, "I still go by and see the one who is doing life."

When William said "doing life" I knew his meaning for those words was different than mine. I used those words quite a bit when I served a church in the suburbs. It was not uncommon for me to say to my congregation, "We are doing life together."

Your perspective changes when you try to understand others before trying to be understood. All of a sudden "doing life" can have a whole other meaning.

"Being With" Gateway

Spending meaningful time with the less fortunate is a gateway for experiencing your next season of spiritual growth. I believe our God honors our efforts to connect with and relate to persons who are in need. Immersing ourselves in the lives of the wounded and exposing our own wounds can lead to transformation. I have seen this type of change in the lives of those who practiced "being with" and I, too, have experienced transformation. When we dare to overcome our fear of being transparent, and choose to "be with," we have an incredible opportunity for a new future in God's Kingdom.

Reflection Questions

1. Have you ever been part of an urban mission project? If so, was the focus "doing for" or "being with" persons?

2. "Ghetto Tourism" is popular. Katie was upset with church groups that drove in, passed out food, took pictures, and left without ever speaking. What would you say to Katie? What advice would you give groups from churches who are interested in participating in "Ghetto Tourism?"

3. What is your biggest challenge to "being with" persons who are different than you?

4. Reread Luke 4:16-30. Why do you think the Jewish leaders in the synagogue ran Jesus out of town?

5. Have you ever spent time with the marginalized? What do you remember about the experience?

6. What can the broken in urban areas teach those who are broken in the suburbs?

Chapter 5

FEAR

"Afraid yet filled with joy." Matthew 28:8

We have spent several chapters discussing how God will use urban missions to precipitate life-changing experiences in the city. By now, if you live in the suburbs, you know there is uncertainty in leaving the comfort of our "burbs" for an immersion experience in the ghetto. The thought of spending an extended amount of time with a group of homeless individuals on their turf can create a certain level of panic and fear. Each time these emotions creep into my thoughts, I am reminded of Paul's encouraging words that we do not have a spirit of fear (Romans 8:15). With that said, fear is real. As a matter of fact, I think some level of fear is healthy, especially if your fear is appropriate.

I have only had one experience, spending time with the marginalized, when I came face to face with legitimate fear.

While Atlanta has many homeless shelters, there is only one Peachtree-Pine Shelter, located on the corner of Peachtree Street and Pine Street. On cold winter nights, this shelter will house 600 to 700 homeless men. The majority of these men are chronically homeless because of drug addiction and mental illness. It is not a safe place. Homeless men have told me they would rather sleep outside than spend a night inside the shelter. I think the number one reason this shelter has such a dangerous reputation is that one does not need an ID for admission. No one is searched for weapons or drugs when entering. Fear and terror live at Peachtree-Pine.

You can imagine my surprise when I heard what I thought was God nudging me to spend a night in Peachtree-Pine. I was serving a Methodist church downtown and the last thing I desired was to spend the night in what many considered to be the most dangerous shelter in the city. After months of trying to avoid the Divine whisper, I set the date and did it. I began a 24-hour fast from my way of life, and lived among the homeless of Atlanta, including spending a night in the infamous shelter.

At approximately 1:00 a.m., I found myself in a maze of homeless men, being chased by one who was high on crack cocaine. He had confronted me moments earlier, telling me he planned to kill me. Fortunately, the bouncers on duty that night intervened and the man was escorted out of the shelter.

The following day as I reflected upon my experience in the shelter, I remembered a quote from Erwin McManus, a pastor in Los Angeles, I had jotted down after hearing him speak many years earlier.

> *"You don't choose when you die but you do get to choose if you live." Erwin McManus*

I share this story to let you know that experiencing fear in the ghetto is real, and often common. Fear is present any time one enters an environment that is known by its crime statistics. With that said, I have never experienced any fear while serving inside the gates of the City of Refuge. If you become afraid, I encourage you to discern if your fear is legitimate.

Fear Can Be Paralyzing

The problem with fear is that sometimes paralysis comes with it. Because of fear, our lives are filled with missed opportunities to participate in the Kingdom. I can look back on my life and see times when fear kept me from obeying God's voice.

This is how my past encounters with fear have played out. I experience what I identify as a holy nudge and think about what the next steps ought to be. Then fear kicks in, causing excuses why I cannot obey God. Consequently, my lack of obedience hinders God using me as He wishes. If this scenario has played out once in my life, it has played out hundreds of times. Fear paralyzes.

Several years ago I joined the YMCA. With membership came an orientation to the gym, including a one-on-one training session from a staff professional. My trainer, Sue, demonstrated how to properly use each machine, then watched as I performed each exercise. She carefully explained what I needed to do and how often I needed to do it. For the last portion of orientation, Sue went over basic dietary rules. By the time she came to fatty foods and bad carbohydrates, I stopped her and said, "Sue, I appreciate all of this information. But you need to know I do not have an information problem. I have an execution problem!"

What I have seen modeled in my own life is that fear keeps me from doing God's will. Most of us know right from wrong. More often than not, we know what God wants us to do with our lives regarding a specific situation. Information is really not the issue.

Executing God's will over our will is our issue.

What we lack is courage to obey God. We allow fear to paralyze us from what we know we ought to do. God's words to Joshua need to be written on our souls: "Be strong and courageous...for the Lord your God will be with you" (Joshua 1:9).

Fear and Parenting

It is a sad thing to see how fear affects our parenting. Over the years several teens in my congregations have expressed an interest in full-time ministry only to have one or both parents respond by saying something like, "I'm okay if you go into ministry, but only after you pursue a degree in business education. You know, the church needs Christians in business to financially support the church." In other words the parent is saying, "I want you to make as much money as you can and church work will not meet the financial expectations I have for you."

When we first launched Restoration ATL, I had a responsible mother ask me several questions regarding her daughter working with the homeless. One of those questions was driven by fear: "Will she be safe? I want her to have the experience of working with the less fortunate but I am a little afraid. Should I be afraid?" It was a fair question. Most of the communities in which we live are relatively safe, but the inner city is different. Fear is a normal response for a suburban mother sending her child into the ghetto. But there should be another type of fear, a fear that will most likely impact her life far more.

More than the fear associated with your child being physically harmed, a greater fear needs to be your child coming back from the ghetto changed for life.

My experience of having introduced suburban youth to urban missions is that God awakens a Kingdom spark within them. He begins a new awareness in their lives. There is a change that happens and I can only imagine how the conversations at home are influenced.

"Mom and Dad, I know I have been planning on being a _____ (Fill in with a profession that equals financial security for you), but I think God wants me to _____ (Fill in with a profession that is more focused on making a difference than economic security)."

The fear of wanting to protect our children from harm can limit our children ever participating in God's work. I know you are rearing your child to "do better" than you, to be a professional, to earn the MBA, to live the "good life," and to carry the family name to the next economic tier. Maybe your goal is for your child to provide for you later in life. I know you have dreams for your children; Beth and I share similar dreams for our sons. Guess what? God may have different plans for our children. Yes, the thought scares me too. Serving in urban ministry is risky. It is possible that one's life could be changed forever. It all begins with facing the fear.

My First Taste of Urban Fear

I was raised in a rural county, about 25 miles south of Atlanta. Throughout my growing up years, the racial makeup of the county was 95 percent white, 4 percent black, and 1 percent others. I graduated from high school and attended a small United Methodist junior college in the mountains of north Georgia and during my two years on campus, we had just three African-Americans students out of a population of four hundred. In my first twenty years of life, I spent limited time with racially different persons.

Then came June 1988, the summer between my sophomore and junior years of college. I entered a Methodist program that placed college students in churches as summer youth directors. After being admitted, we had a week of basic training and then were sent to our summer assignments. While I visualized working with an affluent group of suburban youth in a growing community, God had a different agenda for me. I was a little shocked when the director of the program said: "Jimmy, you are going to work at Camp Wesley in southwest Atlanta, as a summer camp counselor."

Camp Wesley was an abandoned 4-H camp in south Fulton County, which had become a Methodist church camp. The camp served youth from the inner city of Atlanta. Although I had never heard of the place, many assured me it would be a positive experience. As I learned more about Camp Wesley, I think it is fair to say that my inner fear reared its ugly head.

As it turned out, serving as a camp counselor the summer of 1988 would be one of the most pivotal Kingdom experiences in my 25 years of ministry. Of thirteen staff members, I was the only white person. Of the 256 children we hosted at camp through that summer, only six were white. The experience was a revelation for me and at times, culturally shocking. Camp Wesley introduced me to new Kingdom experiences.

Being immersed in a completely different culture caused an enormous amount of personal fear and anxiety. Will I be welcomed? Will I be able to relate? Will I be trusted? Most of my fear was what might be expected from a white, middle class country boy. I had been influenced more by urban television shows than reality. Consequently, my greatest fear should have been how Camp Wesley would forever change my life and my understanding of what it means to participate in the Kingdom of God.

Fear and Joy

Do you remember how Matthew describes the response of the women who first discovered the empty tomb on the first Easter? As the women left to go and to share their discovery with the twelve disciples, Matthew writes, "So the women hurried away from the tomb, afraid yet filled with joy, and ran to tell his disciples" (Matthew 28:8).

"Afraid yet filled with joy" that first Easter. The phrase reminds me that living in God's Kingdom involves both joy and fear. If we are going to live in such a way that we experience the Kingdom in the present, rest assured there will be some fear involved. Even though joy may seem to be present in our lives, seldom will we experience the full abundant life with Jesus without encountering some level of fear and discomfort.

Nowhere in the scriptures are we promised a joy-filled life without working through some level of fear.

I have encountered fear many times over the past 25 years in ministry. The voice of fear spoke loudly the day I showed up at Camp Wesley and realized I was the only white guy around. The same voice whispered in my ear the day I mailed in my admission papers for seminary. Fear was present when I planted a new church, and when I was appointed to serve a downtown congregation. I was terrified when we began a mission to the homeless without any funding, a building, or any people. As I look back on my life, anytime I have tried to build the Kingdom, fear was a factor.

Fear Shaped By Prejudice

Facing the fear that inevitably comes with urban missions is part of the journey. We tote our own insecurities as well as prejudices shaped by our past. Failing to acknowledge this is not only a lack of self-awareness, but also a reflection of our ignorance. When I first found myself immersed in urban ministry, I certainly carried society's stereotypical thinking of middle-class Caucasian people regarding the poor and specifically, homeless African-American people. Sadly, I was quick to judge and thought I had all of the answers as to the reason they were homeless. Fear was the driving force that influenced my lack of understanding.

Our racial and social prejudices run deep and it is a part of what needs to be confronted inside us on a daily basis. Remember Stephen Covey's thought, "Seek first to understand before seeking to be understood." When we fail to acknowledge our own prejudices, fear rules us and makes it convenient to live in shallow relationships of our own choosing. The fear, which stems from prejudices, overlooks seeing other persons as fellow children of the living Lord.

The fear is mutual. Have you ever thought of the fear that the marginalized have of suburban white people or the fear that some urban black women naturally have regarding suburban white men? Working with hundreds of homeless black women has helped me understand why many women in the margins do not trust white men. Fear encourages building walls and keeping relationships at a distance. Just as it is understandable why fear resides in the suburbs, it is just as understandable why fear is present among the urban poor.

I first met Cheryl in the homeless shelter at the City of Refuge. She was kind, interesting, and full of life. She seemed to be well adjusted considering her housing situation. She attended one of our weekend retreats and we immediately began a friendship. Cheryl became an active participant during the RATL retreats and quickly became one of the residents that I depended on to help with our programming. As we spent more and more time together, Cheryl began to open up and one day she shared part of her own story.

"Pastor Jim, when I got here I did not like men or trust any man, specifically white men. My life was fine until a white man sexually assaulted me. That's when things started falling apart for me."

I remember listening to Cheryl's horrific story and questioning the evil within this predator when Cheryl added to her story, "You know Pastor Jim, this place has taught me that it is safe to trust white men again."

*God brings together Kingdom minded
people to deal with the fear they share.*

Breaking Down Fear

Have you considered that God possibly wants to use you to help break down some fear that exists in the lives of those who are broken in the city? The beautiful aspect in this relationship is that God often uses the poor to break down our own fears. For those of us who are white and have been raised outside urban areas, we cannot possibly comprehend the fear that has been instilled in society's poor. Likewise, we do not do a very good job of acknowledging the angst and fear that resides within us. I believe this is one of the reasons why God wants us to immerse ourselves with the broken in the city.

I have come to value the interaction between homeless children in the shelter with older male volunteers. The majority of the children have little to no interaction with their biological fathers. This interaction between suburban fathers and urban children meets deep social, spiritual, and physiological needs for both. It is fun to observe the transformation that takes place.

Brian and his family attended one of our weekend RATL retreats. Brain was a successful business owner who had little contact with urban children in his 40 years. As an upper middle-class, white male living in the suburbs, he found himself in a culture that was unlike anything he had ever experienced.

During a debrief session, we were discussing the issues that a fatherless culture creates and the long-term systemic problems that ultimately follow. I mentioned to Brian that he should not be surprised with the affectionate response he received from the children. I said, "For some of those children, tonight was the first time they had ever laughed and played with a white man. For some, they had never even touched the skin of a white man." Brian interrupted me and said, "Well, until tonight, I've never been this close and spent as much time with black children."

While fear was crumbling,
transformation was taking place.

Fear and Distractions

I have a friend who is a triathlete. You probably have seen these individuals who combine swimming, biking, and running for a workout most would consider insane. I have competed in several mini-triathlons, but my friend is in a different league because he does the longer distances and he is a much stronger athlete.

Recently he was telling me about a trip he took to Florida to visit his relatives. The mini-vacation overlapped with scheduled swim days, so he thought he would enjoy a workout in the lake behind his cousin's home. My friend said all was going well as he explained his intentions until his cousin told him, "That sounds good. Just be aware of the alligator trap on the other side of the cove." As my friend put it, "I knew at that moment the distraction of an alligator trap would prevent my putting a foot into that water!"

Distractions. What keeps you from doing what you know is important? Most of us fight this daily battle of knowing what we ought to do, but not following through.

We know we need to spend more time with our spouse, or with our children, or on that project at work or at school, but often it does not get done. Why? Distractions. We get caught up paying attention to something that hinders what we want to accomplish.

Distractions lead us to majoring in the minors of life.

Distractions are often a catalyst for fear. My experience of having worked in urban missions has taught me that distractions and fear go hand and hand. Often, what we call a distraction is actually a cover-up for a fear. I know this is true when it comes to immersing ourselves in urban work.

I talk to many pastors and church leaders about involving their congregations in inner city missions. The majority of the time, leaders are receptive to hearing how God is working in the city, and the transformation that can take place. They acknowledge the idea that God really does use the broken to heal the broken. However, sometimes I hear a hint of fear in their response.

Larry serves a church in North Atlanta. His church does a great job of providing programs for members, but there are not many opportunities for parishioners to serve in local missions. We were discussing the retreat at the shelter, talking about how families could come to Atlanta and actually be on a spiritual retreat with individuals who were transitioning out of homelessness. He immediately started listing the number of programs the church had going on and how busy his parishioners were with children's sports activities. Then he admitted, "I'm not sure I want my parishioners in the inner city." Fear.

When fear is present, distractions and excuses abound.

Whom Shall I Fear?

When Faith came to the shelter she was wearing colorful ethnic clothing. From her accent, I could tell she was not from the States. When I asked about her heritage, she revealed her native land was Haiti.

Faith shared stories of her childhood and the Christian faith her parents and grandparents had instilled in her. She had an infectious smile and was full of joy. She talked about God's provisions, her blessings and the opportunity God had given her to minister to other women in the shelter. I could see the respect the women in the shelter had for her. Also, her chore on campus was serving meals in the kitchen and I could see the love she showed the women and children. It did not take long for us to become friends.

I distinctly remember a conversation with Faith regarding her future at the shelter. She was facing a deadline for moving and would soon be leaving. Although she had searched for a job, time was running out for her at the shelter. If something did not open for her soon, she would be transferred to another shelter in the city.

I wanted to have a practical, "dose of reality," conversation with Faith. Most of our conversations were spiritual and "Christian" in nature, so I thought a more, "this is about to happen" conversation might be helpful. As we sat down and I began explaining her future she politely interrupted me saying, "Oh Pastor Jim, only God knows my future. God has me. I have no fear. I am a daughter of the King!"

Well, the rest of the story is that God did have Faith in the palm of His hand and today, she has her own place and is doing well. Faith was right all along. I have often reflected upon our conversation, and upon Faith's words of assurance, "God has me and I have no fear whatsoever."

Faith taught me an incredible principle of Christ's Kingdom. If we allow our trust of God to orchestrate our attitudes and actions, we will have nothing to fear at all. As our personal acceptance of God's authority grows, all other fear subsides. When our desire to obey God outweighs the other fears in our lives, we will find ourselves in the midst of life-changing work in God's Kingdom.

Reflection Questions

1. When did you experience fear as a child? What do you remember about that experience of fear?
2. How do you cope with fear? Share a time when you overcame a fear?
3. Fear is often paralyzing. Can you think of a time when fear kept you from doing something God was leading you to do? Explain.
4. As you think about serving in inner city missions, what fears and reservations do you have? What do you think is the root of our fears?
5. Do you think Faith was naive? What can we take away from Faith's story?
6. What can you do this week to help face your fear of trusting God completely?

BROKEN TO BROKEN

Chapter 6

PRUNING

*"Every branch that does bear fruit he prunes
so that it will be even more fruitful." John 15:2*

The "S" WORD

One of my favorite television sitcoms is "The Andy Griffith Show." Do you remember the episode when the visiting preacher came to Mayberry? The scene I recall from that episode is Barney commenting on the preacher's sermon when he says, "Yes sir, that's one subject you just can't talk enough about: sin." I laugh every time I think of Barney's awkwardness, but the scene is a reminder of how awkward the topic of sin actually is.

Since Genesis 3, sin has affected our fruitfulness in the Kingdom. Where there is disobedience to God, growth of his Kingdom is hindered. Adam and Eve experienced it, and thousands of years later, it is still true. Sin destroys what God has created. Every one you meet could share a story of the negative impact of sin.

We do not talk much about sin in our culture. As a matter of fact, I thought about leaving this chapter out of the book after a colleague joked, "Sin? Why do you want to include a chapter on something we all know about?" Why is it important to use the "S" word when discussing urban missions? How we deal with sin in our lives affects how God will use us to produce fruit for His sake. The human condition is sinful, and if sin in our lives is not addressed, the Kingdom is negatively impacted.

The problem with sin is: we accept that our sin may affect us, but tell ourselves that it does not impact those around us, or those we want to serve. If you have had this conversation with yourself, I have a challenge for you. Assume your sin does affect others and see how pruning that sin from your life impacts your fruitfulness in the Lord. As much as we do not want to admit it, our sin impacts our effectiveness for the Kingdom.

I am a believer in grace. I know firsthand how experiencing forgiveness from God and others can make you feel like you have a new life. I have been the recipient of grace throughout my life and I am champion of proclaiming God's grace to our broken world! Dietrich Bonhoeffer, a German minister who died in a concentration camp, said, "Cheap grace is the grace we bestow on ourselves. Cheap grace is the preaching of forgiveness without requiring repentance..." Hanging our hat on God's grace without dealing with our sin cheapens our relationship with our Lord, and with others.

God is in the business of redeeming our past for his glory, if we choose to partner with Him. Each time I find myself in a dark emotional place, I am comforted by David's hopeful words, "God redeems my life from the pit" (Psalm 103:4).

God's desire is to redeem our past sin for His glory.

If you are in a spiritual pit due to sin, this season of life can be a nail in your spiritual coffin, or it can help you grow and make a larger impact for Christ. While sin hinders our Kingdom influence, believing your sin is unredeemable is just as sinful. Believing that sin prevents you from being part of God's plan is a lie of the devil.

Choosing not to turn away from sin keeps us in the pit of sin. Praying for God to remove us from a dark place, to give us relief and peace while we continue to live in sin, is pointless. Choosing not to prune is spiritually binding, while pruning is just the opposite. Removing that which hinders our spiritual journey, leads to hope and renewal. Pruning opens a spiritual path for growth.

Sadly, I have known too many who have gone to their grave after refusing to deal with a dark place in their past. By living our lives in the shadows of past decisions, we will not finish our life's course well. God has the power to redeem our sin because that is the business of God. Broken does not mean useless.

The Dump

Our boys like retrieving what others discard. Both of them have a fascination with picking through what others want to give away, throw away or sell for pennies on the dollar. Shopping at yard sales, going to thrift stores, and even stopping to see what others have left by the side of the road, is part of their routine. From the time when they were very young, Will and Ben looked forward to going on an "adventure" to our local dump. I am hesitant to admit it, but my boys would tell you these trips were highlights of their early years!

One Saturday, the boys and I made a trip to the county dump to drop off old batteries for recycling and several pieces of decrepit furniture for the trash pile. As we drove into the dumping area, there was a long line of pick-up trucks and SUVs pulling trailers, waiting their turn to unload. If you have ever made a run to the dump, you know the routine: back up to the pile, unload quickly, and move on. There is not any time to waste, and someone is always waiting for you to get out of the way. This particular day was no different, except that the stench was pretty strong stuff!

Our dump trip was going smoothly until it was time to "move on." Seven-year-old Will was in the back of the truck helping me unload, but as we were hauling off the last of the furniture, I noticed Ben was nowhere to be found. Our four-year-old had wandered off and, although I knew he could not have gone very far, a little panic set in.

"BEN, BEN!" I yelled. Within a few moments, I heard a familiar voice say, "Dad, look up here!" Ben had climbed to the top of a dump pile and was sitting on an old, disgustingly filthy couch with his legs crossed and his arm resting on the back like a pirate who had found his treasure.

"Ben, get down from there. That couch is nasty. No telling what has been on it and may be in it right now!"

"Dad, can we take it home with us? We can put it in our hut outside. I know it needs cleaning but we can clean it up. We can get rid of these stains. We can still use it!"

You will be relieved to know we did not take it home, even though both boys thought the sofa would be a good addition to the "treasures" they had collected over the years. However, their desire to take home that stained, torn, and stinking couch so they could clean it up and use it, served as a wonderful illustration for me. As I have reflected on that day, the scene is a beautiful expression of our spiritual journeys, and what it means for us to live in Christ's Kingdom.

In the midst of our stained, soiled, and dirty lives, we serve a God who longs for us to come back home with Him. His desire is to clean us up for His glory.

Jesus On Pruning

We have a tendency to focus on God's grace without considering God's desire to prune sin from our lives. Pruning is part of our Christian life, and if we expect to be used as God intends, repentance and change are necessary.

In John 15, when our Lord's earthly life neared its end, Jesus shared these words with his disciples: "I am the true vine, and my Father is the gardener. He cuts off every branch in me that bears no fruit, while every branch that does bear fruit he prunes so that it will be even more fruitful" (John 15:1-2).

It may seem like an oxymoron, but pruning and growth go hand in hand. Just as trees and shrubs are pruned at the end of the season so they will come back stronger the next year, pruning is part of the growth process that we experience as followers of Jesus. It is important to note that pruning is reserved for those who are already bearing fruit, rather than those who are "dead on the vine." Jesus mandates pruning for those of us who are laboring in his Kingdom, so we can make an even larger impact for Christ.

The biblical concept of pruning is not a popular topic. It is easier to discuss God's promises of blessings and favor than it is to discuss discarding sin and seeking God's cleansing touch. Pruning that which comes between you and your relationship with our Heavenly Father deepens your understanding of your effectiveness in his Kingdom.

Own What Needs Pruning

Through personal experience and counseling others, I have learned that if we do not own our sin, we fall short in living the life God desires for us. Our relationships with God, and our relationship with those we love may be hindered and spiritual decay can set in.

Owning our sin and pruning sin is freeing. The only way I know how to move on from sin in a healthy way is to own it, claim it, prune it, and ask God to redeem it and me for His glory as I move forward. I do not intend to simplify what can be extremely complicated, but I can tell you that it works. I am sure you know individuals who have not really owned their sin, and they seem stuck in life. You may be living in a season where you have not taken responsibility for your sin. I have certainly been there. It is sad to see and even sadder to live.

Admitting failure is difficult and pride keeps us from saying: "I am sorry. I messed up. What I did hurt you and was wrong in God's eyes." Acknowledging and taking responsibility for actions that led you to where you are is painful because of pride.

We are a stubborn people. We want what we want and we want it now. We do not do well with the word "no," and we are very uncomfortable admitting we are broken vessels, lugging our pasts like baggage. We want the world to revolve around us while not being accountable for our selfish ways. Sound familiar? Sin and brokenness are inevitable when pride abounds.

You're Not My Boss!

When our boys were young, we lived across the street from a family with two girls very close in age to Will and Ben. Our families shared many good times. Most days Betsy, Meredith, Will, and Ben would find something to explore or to do around the house or in the neighborhood.

Betsy, the oldest girl, had a tendency to mother her little sister, so it was always fun to watch whenever there was a dispute between them. Meredith wanted to lead the activity, or make a decision on behalf of the group, and Betsy would correct her or tell her she would have to wait. Meredith's response was always the same, "You are not my boss! You can't boss me around. YOU ARE NOT MY BOSS!"

How many times have we thought those same words to ourselves after being told something needed changing in our lives? How many times have we made the same statement to God and continued rebelling against him? We do not like obeying the boss, do we? We like doing what we want to do, without any accountability. Sadly, our pride keeps us from acknowledging that we need to answer to someone other than ourselves. We are accountable to Almighty God so when he says something needs pruning, the quickest way for growth and, ultimately for peace, is pruning.

Pruning Past Wounds

Letting go of bitterness or regret associated with a painful past is hard. It is difficult to hold on to pain from years back and still experience the spiritual freedom of Kingdom living. Of all of the difficult topics I have listened to during counseling sessions, emotional sufferings due to the sin of another tops the list. I have listened to hundreds of stories from individuals who have suffered due to the sinful decisions of a spouse, parent, sibling, or close friend.

I was shocked when Kim pulled me aside following a worship service one Sunday and asked if she could come by the church office to see me. Kim was married with three beautiful children; she and her family had been visiting the church for several months. That morning, I could tell from the look in Kim's eyes that she was in deep stress and pain.

"I hate him and I always will. What he did to me is unforgivable and I will never forgive him." Kim's anger and passion were palpable as she sat in my office and told me stories of the emotional and physical abuse she endured from her father. The previous Sunday I had preached a sermon on forgiveness, and my sermon point was *Forgiveness leads to Freedom*. I mentioned in the message how choosing not to forgive hinders the level of freedom you will experience as a follower of Christ. If we cannot forgive, we allow ourselves to be emotional captives. My message hit a nerve with Kim and she was letting me know how she felt.

"Kim, I do not pretend to understand the level of pain you are experiencing because of your father's sin. I do know the pain you are carrying with you is preventing you from experiencing peace and hindering what God can do in your life. I am not suggesting you become reconciled with your father or even to make any contact, but I do believe it would be healthy to ask God to give you the strength to put your father's sin in the past so that you can move forward. Can you forgive him and move forward?"

"No. I can not forgive him, and I do not plan asking God to help me forgive him."

I wish Kim's story had ended differently. I wish she could have let go of the heavy burden of bitterness and move on with her life. But, moving past deep pain is not easy for most of us.

Louise

Louise regularly attended worship when she was a resident at the City of Refuge. Worship is a focal point for many of the residents during their tenure at the shelter, and Louise never missed. Once you attend a RATL worship service, you experience how powerful it is. The residents will tell you they could not make it without these services, and I have also grown dependent on these worship experiences. I look forward to our worship times at the shelter because they have become a venue for God to speak clearly into my soul.

Louise would be the first to tell you RATL worship services were a source of strength and comfort for her at the City of Refuge. As a single mom, her life has been layered with hardships and difficulties. Single parenting is challenging enough, however, raising children alone in the inner city adds enormous challenges. Rearing children in a culture where crime is rampant, accepted, and even encouraged often means watching them suffer. Some of Louise's stories of the gangs and violence her teenage sons were caught up in would make the hair on my neck stand up.

Louise finished praying at the altar one evening at the close of a RATL service where I had preached on identifying your spiritual roadblocks and asking God to remove them for us. Louise was struggling with forgiveness.

"Pastor Jim, I know I need to forgive him but it is so hard."

"Tell me more, Louise. Why are you struggling with forgiving this person?"

Through her tears Louise said, "Pastor Jim, he killed my son. It was all gang-related, but he did not have to kill him. I am just having a hard time forgiving him. The memory of Leonard being shot haunts me. I know that I am supposed to forgive the boy who pulled the trigger but..."

This was no time for a theological discussion; it was a time for being. This was a time for seeking God's healing touch in the midst of deep pain. We sat down and cried together.

Almost every weekend I remind the volunteers who participate on the spiritual retreats we have much to learn from the residents in the shelter. This particular evening, God was using Louise to speak to my own life. Louise was modeling what it means to live in the Kingdom. As I witnessed her pain, God was nudging me to do some pruning in my own life.

Pruning and Peace

As difficult as pruning can be, nothing will free your soul from captivity like discarding sin from your life. Nothing will lead to more growth. Nothing will lead to more peace. There is freedom in casting off that which interferes with your relationships with God and with those you love. Acknowledging the need for pruning, and following through with it opens doors for Kingdom opportunities.

God honors our lives when we prune and gives us peace only he can grant.

Final Thoughts on Pruning

I included this chapter on pruning because I have seen the positive impact of removing sin from my life. I am convinced the degree of our Kingdom influence is directly related to our ability to prune that which interferes with our relationship with God. Most importantly, pruning improves the health of our souls.

Some of us are addicted to power, prestige, and wealth. Some of us deal with sexual or substance addiction. Some of us are caught in the addiction of trying to appear as if we have no addictions at all. Each of us deals with demons that damage our relationship with God and those around us. These addictions and sins will ultimately bankrupt our souls and paralyze us in our Kingdom work. This is why pruning is critical for the follower of Jesus interested in growing spiritually and becoming more Christ-like.

The irony is, when we acknowledge our brokenness in the midst of our pruning, God places us to help others who are in need of pruning. The Kingdom principle is true: God uses the broken to help heal the broken. Reflect on this critical question:

What in my life needs pruning today so that God can use me, a deeply wounded and broken person myself, to help another broken person?

Reflection Questions

1. Most of us understand the concept of pruning when it comes to gardening. Have you ever failed to prune a tree or shrub that needed it? What happened?

2. Read John 15:1-2. According to Jesus, who is the gardener? Who is the vine? Who is the branch? Who needs pruning? Why is pruning necessary?

3. To prune is to trim dead vines or limbs. Can you think of a time when you removed something from your life that was a spiritual hindrance and you became more productive? How does this concept of removing or pruning impact our spiritual well-being?

4. Can you think of a time when you resisted pruning something from your life that was negatively impacting your relationship with God? You read the story of a woman who chose not to forgive her father. Why do we struggle with forgiving people who have wronged us?

5. Spiritual pruning leads to spiritual growth. When was a time in your life that you experienced a surge in your spiritual life? Did pruning precede your growth?

6. Identify one thing (addiction, attitude, habit, sin) that is hindering your relationship with God.

Chapter 7

CONTENTMENT

"He restores my soul." Psalms 23:3

Contentment is something very few of us experience. Our lack of fulfillment is a result of the ways we seek to restore our depleted souls. We try to fix our brokenness through consumerism and the relationships we use for our own gain. It is our human condition to seek healing from sources we control or provide, rather than seeking restoration from Almighty God. The world is quick to provide imitations that lure us into believing that fulfillment, satisfaction, and contentment can be found in something other than Kingdom living. This is the very reason why serving, and spending quality time with the marginalized and wounded, is critical if we expect to find rest and peace for our souls.

Imitations

I have a good friend, Richard, who recently restored a 1968 Cutlass convertible that was headed to the junkyard. New, this car was a beauty. With a candy apple red exterior, black leather interior, and mag wheels, this car was a head-turner! In its day, this vehicle was top of the line. However, by the time Richard purchased it, there was nothing pretty about it. The only thing it had going for it was possibility.

While he was restoring the car, I learned from Richard there are companies that sell original car parts for the purpose of restoring vehicles. These companies produce magazines with pages and pages of parts for sale. Those who purchase from these companies do not want imitation parts; they want their vehicles restored with original manufactured parts. Because my friend is a purist, he used such a company on his now fully-restored 1968 beauty.

Richard told me something interesting about some of the companies selling parts for car restoration projects: "Jimmy, you have to know the company where you buy the parts. You need to go to the right source for what you need. If you do not know the source, it is likely you will buy an imitation part."

Sound familiar? I know there are many of us who do not go to the right source when it comes to seeking restoration for our souls. As spiritual beings, we will find fulfillment in the midst of our faith journeys while seeking a deeper, and hopefully more meaningful relationship with Jesus Christ. Too many of us compromise and seek joy, peace, and happiness in ways that are counterproductive to our relationship with the Almighty. As a result, we end up fighting through fatigue, discouragement, and depression. We fall into the trap of believing the contented life does not exist, so we numb our souls and seek satisfaction through short-term thrills. Our daily tasks and relationships become shallow which leaves us experiencing emptiness and ultimately compromising how God created us to live.

Contentment is replaced with compromise.

Psalms 23 is a favorite scripture for many and if you grew up in the church, chances are you have this familiar psalm memorized. My favorite part of the psalm is verse 3: "He restores my soul." That one verse is a reminder of the broken condition of our souls, and the need for personal restoration. It also reminds us that God is the source of our restoration.

Blowing Bubbles

I have friends who are avid divers and they are "all in," literally! Diving is more than a hobby for this family; it is part of their DNA and most members of their immediate and extended family are certified divers. Family vacations with grandparents, children, and grandchildren are usually to exotic dive spots around the world. This family comes together to enjoy the deep blue wonders of God's creation because of Bill.

Bill, the patriarch of the family, introduced each of his children and grandchildren to the sport of diving. As a certified diving instructor, it was natural for Bill to teach each member of the family everything one needs to know about diving. Though diving is now a focal point for this family, not all family members were "all in" from the beginning.

Although one grandchild was acquiring a diving certification, she was a little timid about exploring the ocean depths with her parents and cousins. No matter what words of encouragement she received from family members, she would not venture out into deeper waters. Her grandfather, who continued to provide reassurance and instruction, had grown short on patience when he said, "Ashton! You need to make a choice. Are you going to spend your time blowing bubbles, or are you going deep with the rest of us?"

We face a choice in our faith journeys. We can choose to live either in the shallows, not venturing beneath the surface in our relationship with Jesus Christ, or we can dive deeper, taking our faith journey to a place where spiritual contentment can be found. Deep fulfillment and satisfaction in life cannot be found living on the surface, "blowing bubbles." Contentment is found in seeking greater depth with God, pursuing the Kingdom in every aspect of our lives. It can be risky seeking the Kingdom since God may call you outside your comfort zone, but it is the only way to find contentment in the midst of the journey.

I am reminded of Jesus' words, "Come to me, all you who are weary and burdened, and I will give you rest" (Matthew 11:28). Jesus offers contentment, peace, and rest to those who first come to him.

*Rest for one's soul begins with
coming to Jesus, the Rest Giver.*

Contentment Paradox

In his book, Purpose Driven Life, Rick Warren writes, "It's not about you." God did not design us to live self-centered lives. We should not be self-absorbed, constantly seeking to please only ourselves with wants and desires that ultimately leave us empty. It is not about you or me, yet you and I seeking contentment is all about us. Discovering contentment is a Kingdom paradox.

Contentment is discovered through serving others.

According to Jesus, living in the Kingdom involves discovering a life of fullness and completeness by serving others (Matthew 25:31-46). God created us to experience a joy-filled life as we serve others in the name of Christ. We experience Christ, who offers us contentment, in the midst of serving others. The paradox of the abundant life is that we experience personal fulfillment when we live beyond ourselves. When life is not about us, we find the joy, peace, and fulfillment for which so many are searching. Jesus wants us to discover contentment, true peace, and genuine rest for our souls, but we will not discover that true contentment until we start living for something greater than ourselves.

Power Cling

No modern spiritual writer has impacted my life more than Henri Nouwen. He understood and articulated beautifully in his writings that contentment was not found in winning, not being first and foremost, but rather in serving and seeking to learn from the least of these. He wrote, "Keep your eyes on the prince of peace, the one who doesn't cling to his divine power." Clinging to our own power and using that power for self gain keeps us from experiencing the contented life. Jesus perfectly modeled how to be powerful while not using it for self; his power was used for the sake of the Kingdom.

Jesus experienced contentment because he kept his eyes on the Father and his purposes. Even though we know this is the formula for contentment in our own lives, we continue to cling to the power that we mistakenly think we possess. We are so immersed in trying to maintain or to increase our own authority that we become calloused to the needs of others.

Keeping our eyes on ourselves is
not a formula for contentment.

One of the ways we cling to our power is through consumerism, the greatest challenge facing the church today. Satan has used our ability to purchase what we want, when we want it, as a destructive blow to the local church. Consumerism is the ultimate response of taking care of self-wants and desires. We want what we want, and we will use our many resources to fulfill our desires.

Our power to choose and to purchase creates a market where we are the focus. If we are not pleased with a product or service, we find another one to replace it. Clinging to the power that we possess twists our understanding of what it means to be content, which is why spending time with the marginalized plays such an important part in our spiritual growth. When our actions and attitudes are focused on others, there is less time to focus upon self. There is power in letting go of the superficial and temporary to embrace the meaningful and spiritual.

One Sunday following worship, I was standing in the church courtyard greeting worshippers when a first time guest approached me with an interesting request. Our conversation went something like this:

"Pastor, our family really enjoyed the service."

"I am glad you did. How did you hear about the church?"

"A friend of ours invited us to attend. By the way, I have a seven-year-old daughter. Do you have a soccer league for that age group?"

"We do not offer a soccer league here at the church. However, we do have a Sunday School class for your daughter."

The mom smiled, turned and walked away and never came back.

The reality is, I could have responded differently and given her hope that I would look into starting a church youth soccer league. I could have said, "What a great idea! Give me your name and number, and I will follow up about our church starting one." If I had responded that way, she and her family might have come back. But I did not and consequently, I never saw the family again.

Later that afternoon as I reflected upon that conversation, I felt a touch of guilt that I was so quick to respond. My short interaction with the suburban mom also made me reflect on how consumerism has infiltrated the local church. The solution to consumerism in the church is finding contentment by connecting with the marginalized within our reach.

My Next Splurge

The spiritual retreat Restoration ATL offers at City of Refuge ends with the questions: "What is next for you? What has God revealed about your own life? How do you plan on taking what you have experienced this weekend back home? How has the experience changed you?" While everyone's context varies, and implementing the "power of with" back home looks different for each group, the consistent result is an altered perspective on personal comfort and consumerism.

Karen attended a RATL weekend retreat with a group of students from her local church. As an adult chaperone, she observed the change that took place in the lives of the students and within her own soul. During our final debriefing, Karen had everyone's attention after she commented, "I am feeling a little guilty."

"I knew the weekend would change me, but I had no idea the impact would be so powerful. Earlier this morning I started daydreaming about what my next splurge would be. Would I go to Starbucks? Would I go shopping? Would I call a group of my friends for lunch or dinner? Then it dawned on me. My new friends here at the shelter do not have that option. They cannot just decide to go out on the town and enjoy a fun-filled night. And then my guilt surfaced. Here I was planning my next personal indulgence because I had altered my schedule, given up my creature comforts, and had lived in a shelter for one weekend. I am planning my next splurge while my new friends at the shelter are planning how they can transition out of homelessness. I felt dirty having those thoughts. I know indulging myself does not lead to the peace of God I want and desire. Finding contentment really is about investing in relationships, not stuff."

Karen's words struck a chord with those of us sitting around the circle that morning. Most of us admitted that we had similar thoughts. We had chosen to give up our comfortable suburban lifestyles for a weekend to live in a shelter with homeless women and children, and already we were planning our next splurge. Having such a thought is normal; however, we deceive ourselves when we believe contentment comes with our next indulgence. I have had many emails from weekend retreat volunteers describing the positive impact being with residents in the shelter had on their lives.

BROKEN TO BROKEN

Once we connect with the marginalized, we acquire a taste of true contentment and our lives are never the same.

Reflection Questions

1. Can you describe a season of your life when you experienced contentment? What do you attribute to discovering that level of fulfillment?
2. Describe a time when you were seeking contentment only to be disappointed?
3. Contentment comes through serving others. Have you found that to be true? Can you think of a time when serving others did not leave you feeling fulfilled? If so, why?
4. Followers of Christ know that fulfillment and contentment come through Kingdom living. What makes us look outside the Kingdom for happiness?
5. Read Psalms 23:1-3. How is God restoring your soul?
6. How will you seek contentment this week?

Chapter 8

GO!

"Therefore go..." Matthew 28:19

The night that changed everything was January 1, 2013. My wife, Beth, and I had tickets to the Passion Conference in Atlanta. Every year the conference attracts thousands of college students from all over the country for several days of worship experiences that challenge their generation to not be silent in Kingdom work. Although Beth and I were more than twice the age of the 60,000 students who had gathered for the conference, we sat with other "old folks" in a special section.

The previous year had been one of deep grief for me. I had left pastoral ministry after more than two decades of serving in the local church and was struggling to find my way. I knew God was calling me to something more but I did not know what that more was. I was fighting depression and searching for hope. I did not want God to be done using me for his Kingdom purposes. All was not well with my soul.

It was the first night of Passion and the Georgia Dome was rocking. Keep in mind I have attended multiple sporting events and concerts in Georgia's largest arena, and none of those previous experiences matched the level of energy in the room that first night of the conference. Chris Tomlin was leading music and Louie Giglio would deliver the evening's message. God had orchestrated the perfect Kingdom storm to give me hope and begin the healing process for my broken soul.

Tomlin finished leading music and Giglio walked onto the platform. I could sense a strong presence of the Holy Spirit in the room while 60,000 people waited in silence to hear what God had in store for them. Louie announced that his message was based in Ezekiel 37, the story of the dry bones coming back to life. I had preached on the same passage several times over the past twenty years, so I knew the passage well; however, at that point in the evening, I never dreamed God would use Louie Giglio and Ezekiel 37 to change my life forever.

"What once was dead is now alive," Louie articulated the point of his message with clarity and conviction. He said, as believers, each of us must choose life and allow the Spirit of God to engulf us. Louie's message that night was a wake-up call for me. I had been living in the valley way too long and it was time for the Spirit of God to do a new work in my life. God was calling me to more and my "more" meant getting back into ministry, specifically with the broken. I left the Georgia Dome that night with a new passion and calling. This would be the year my "dry bones" would come back to life.

On January 2, 2013, I wrote the following words in my journal, "In 2013 I'm getting back in. I'm not sure what it will look like, but the new ministry will be in Atlanta working with the poor, and somehow involve Ezekiel 37. This will be the year!"

I spent January praying and seeking godly counsel from trusted friends. I could not get this new ministry off my mind. I found myself searching for Kingdom answers to my Kingdom questions. God was doing a new work within my soul, and I knew 2013 would be unlike any previous year of my life. Within a few weeks, God was giving shape to this new vision.

On February 17, 2013, for the first time, the name "Restoration ATL" appeared in my prayer journal. Restoration would be our focus. We would seek to help the marginalized in the city experience restoration. The other side of that coin was that restoration would also take place in the lives of those who would come into the city to serve. From my time serving a congregation in downtown Atlanta, I had firsthand knowledge that the poorest sections in the city were in need of restoration and serving in the suburbs revealed the need for restoration as well. Most importantly, I was aware of my own need for spiritual restoration. God had given me the name, Restoration ATL, for this new ministry.

I immediately began putting together a ministry strategy for Restoration ATL. Every free second I could find, I worked on capturing ideas for this new mission. Restoration ATL would not be like the traditional inner-city urban mission. The focus would not be "doing for," but rather, "being with." I accumulated several pages of ideas and the plan was coming together.

I used blank pieces of paper and a pen to capture most of my ideas for the ministry plan. When you write the word Restoration, what seems like hundreds of times over a few weeks, you quickly realize that it is a rather long word. To help, I started to abbreviate Restoration ATL with the letters RATL. It was a quick and simple way to get more of my thoughts on paper faster. I never dreamed God was about to reveal Himself in a new and powerful way through those four letters.

One afternoon during the last week of February, eight weeks after the night Beth and I attended the Passion Conference in Atlanta, our son, Ben, and a friend of his walked into my home office to say hello. On top of my desk were pages and pages of ideas for Restoration ATL. Ben's friend looked down at my notes and asked, "Mr. Jim, what's up with rattle?"

"What? What are you talking about?"

"Rattle. Look—R-A-T-L."

At that precise moment, I knew God's hand was in Restoration ATL. I knew I had heard God correctly when he said, "GO! 2013 will be the year you will get back in ministry with the poor." I immediately picked up my Bible and went straight to Ezekiel 37. This was the passage God had given me as part of the vision eight weeks earlier. I started to read silently, my heart pounding in my ears.

Then he (God) said to me (Ezekiel), "Prophesy to these bones and say to them, 'Dry ones, hear the word of the Lord! This is what the Sovereign Lord says to these bones: I will make breath enter you, and you will come to life. I will attach tendons to you and make flesh come upon you and cover you with skin; I will put breath in you, and you will come to life. Then you will know that I am the Lord.'"
So I prophesied as I was commanded. And as I was prophesying, there was a noise, a rattling sound, and the bones came together, bone to bone." Ezekiel 37:4-7

As I read the words, "there was a noise, a rattling sound" chill bumps covered my body. God was affirming RATL and I knew in that moment God was opening Kingdom doors for this vision he had given me.

I share this story with you to encourage you to not settle for the mundane. Do not allow fear to keep you from pursuing the dreams God has placed in your heart. For most of us, it takes very little effort to stay comfortable with our current lifestyle. The focus of this last chapter is about taking action. It is a call to Kingdom action. It is about stretching and trusting God to provide for your Kingdom dreams. In one word, "GO!"

Chris

I sat across the table from Chris listening to his story. He was from rural Georgia and had attended Georgia Tech. After graduation, he began working for a large company in Atlanta and within a few years, left to start his own business. In the meantime, he married and began his family. Both his family and the business grew; within a few short years, the business had taken off and he sold the company.

Chris and his family attended a RATL retreat a few months earlier and God was working in his life in a new way. He had been a believer for years. His parents had raised him in the church, and he would say he had maintained an active faith journey since leaving home. But Chris was searching for something more. He knew God was leading him. He just did not know where. When his family attended RATL, we connected and started a friendship. As we caught up with each other over lunch, I was listening to

Chris work through a wonderful dilemma. What do you do with your life when you have access to resources and time?

Chris was living the American Dream! He had a beautiful family, lived in one of Atlanta's most affluent communities, and had plenty of money in the bank. Life was good. But Chris was searching for his next step. He was wise enough to know that playing golf five days a week was not the life God desired for him.

As I listened to more of his story, Chris made a statement that jarred me. He said, "Pastor Jim, I do not want to squander my life. I do not want to get to the end and realize I have wasted what God has given me." WOW! I immediately pulled out my journal and captured the thought.

*How many of us are in danger of
squandering Kingdom opportunities?*

Sadly, I have seen too many examples of lives that were squandered. How would your life change if you decided to make a conscious effort to make a Kingdom difference? How would you need to reallocate your time and resources? As believers, you and I both want to finish life well. All it takes is action on our part.

Steven

Steven had not regularly attended church for more than four decades. Other than the occasional Christmas Eve or Easter service to hear his wife sing in the choir, Steven had no connection with a local congregation. He left the church after his teen years and never looked back.

Although Steven's wife never missed Sunday worship, this was the first time I had met her husband. As I introduced myself, Steven abruptly interrupted and said, "I know who you are, Preacher. But you do not know me. I don't do church." Although we had never met, it did not take long for us to connect. His brashness did not offend, but rather, challenged me to connect with him. There was something about him I really liked.

Steven had been a successful businessman and at fifty-five, was now retired. Steven appeared to be enjoying life but I could sense something was missing for him. After a few minutes of hearing part of his story, I began to probe.

"Why not give the church another try? Come on back."

"Preacher, I already told you I don't do church."

"I hear you. I would not come back either if I didn't think the messages were relevant. I do wish you would try once again. However, if you do decide to come back, wait until I finish preaching our current series. It is not for novices of the faith. It may be too much for you."

You guessed it. Steven showed up the following Sunday, and within weeks he was in a Bible study, participating in local missions, and connecting with the marginalized. Steven will tell you what God has done and continues to do a new work in his life. Why? Because Steven made the decision to no longer be idle in his faith. Steven made a decision to "GO!"

Are you currently idling in your faith?

Growing in Christ's Kingdom involves moving forward, going, stepping out, and opening doors God places before us. Our temptation is to coast or worst yet, become dormant and stagnant in our faith journeys. Living in the mundane is easy. God calls us to so much more. God calls us to "GO!" As followers of Jesus, we do not have the option of retiring from the Kingdom life.

Ed

Ed Nelson has been a spiritual guide and friend of mine since birth. He baptized me as an infant, and has walked along side me for more than four decades. He, his wife Ann, and their children are like family to me. It is hard to express in words the Kingdom impact he has had on my life. You can imagine how honored and humbled I was when he and Ann chose to become part of the congregation I was serving as Ed entered retirement from pastoring in the United Methodist Church. At first, I was a little intimated with Ed and Ann in the congregation on Sundays. Ed was a clergyman with more than forty years of experience in ministry and I was not even forty at the time.

Ed has always had a heart for the underdogs, the leftovers, and the castaways in society. He marched in the Civil Rights Movement when it was not the "in" thing to do. In his more than four decades of full-time ministry, he visited more prisons and jails than any pulpit preacher I know. Every small town in Georgia has a town drunk, and in every small town where Ed pastored, he was that drunk's best friend. Ed understands being with and connecting with the marginalized. This is one of the reasons I love him like I do.

When I was the pastor of Atlanta First United Methodist Church, we offered an annual mission conference, which focused on local urban ministry. Our first year hosting the event, we invited Trevor Hudson to be our guest keynote speaker. Trevor serves on a pastoral team at

Northfield Methodist Church in Binoni, a community near Johannesburg, South Africa. Trevor knows well the sin and ugliness of South African Apartheid and has worked hard to bring together all people in his splintered homeland. Ed and Trevor naturally connected at a deep level. They were, as we say in the South, "two peas in a pod."

Trevor led us in a beautiful way during the conference. He challenged us to examine how we encounter our suffering neighbors and specifically, how these encounters shape us into becoming compassionate Christ-followers. Ed did not miss one session of the conference. Before the conference had ended, God was speaking to Ed and crafting a new mission for him. I was not surprised when Ed asked to see me the day after the conference ended.

"Preacher, I have an idea. The Good Lord has been speaking to me these past few days through Trevor. I am being pushed to spend more time with our suffering neighbors in the city."

Ed went on to explain that he planned to spend Holy Week, which fell two weeks following the mission conference, on the front steps of the church, connecting with the disfranchised within reach of the church doors. With two chairs, a table, a set of checkers, and a sign that read "Free Conversations," Ed made his mission station at 360 Peachtree Street in downtown Atlanta during the holiest week of the Christian year. Ed will tell you the experience challenged and changed him to become more like Jesus.

"I am being pushed to spend more time with our suffering neighbors in the city."

Where is God leading and pushing you? Who within your reach is suffering? I believe God is consistently providing Kingdom-building opportunities along our paths. If we do not hear God it is not because he is not speaking. It is because we are not tuned in to listen for him. Take notice how God is trying to capture your attention.

Almost

Almost. The word reeks of failure.

I have a friend who describes the first season of his life with that word. He was almost a good son. He was almost a good student. He almost had the right job. He almost had his life together to the point that he was going to make a difference and add value to the Kingdom. My friend will tell you that disappointment always accompanies a life defined by "almost."

I can certainly look within my own life and see where I have practiced my personal version of "almost." Too often I have played the "safe card" and not followed that holy nudge that would have led me to deeper waters, to loving God and others more deeply. I have learned the hard way that the "almost" life is laced with regret. You do not want to be defined in any way by "almost."

Does your life have any traces of almost? Chances are you too have experienced seasons where "almost" defined your life. It is not uncommon for us to have lived a life laced with "would've, should've, and could've." We know what the almost life feels like.

Jesus was not a fan of almost. As matter of fact, he told one group of believers that being "lukewarm" was cause to be removed altogether from the Kingdom (Revelation 3:15-16). Jesus does not intend for our lives to be defined by almost. One cannot play life safe, where comfort is the norm, and also be growing the Kingdom. Safe and comfort are hallmarks of the almost life.

Choose today to exchange almost
and safe with joy and fulfillment.

Time to "GO!"

Jesus' Great Commission, recorded in Matthew 28, is a directive from our Lord to "Go and make disciples" (28:19). It is not a suggestion. Jesus does not give us multiple choices from which to choose. If we plan on fulfilling our role in the Kingdom, our first step is to go. A stagnant faith life will not suffice. Action is a requirement.

Have you ever thought that perhaps God has more work he wants you to accomplish? Today is a blank sheet ready for you to write the next chapter of your faith journey. God is waiting for us to "GO!" He is waiting on us to start moving. It is time to "GO!"

One Last Thought

I wrote this book with the premise that God uses broken people to help bring healing to other broken people. God has revealed his healing touch in my life through connecting with other bruised and damaged individuals. Every ounce of healing I have experienced has come as a result of God intervening in my life, primarily through other fragmented souls.

I invite you to "GO!" I encourage you to connect others who are broken within your reach. You can come to Atlanta on a retreat with Restoration ATL or go somewhere closer to your home. Either way, make the decision to "GO!" Take action. God wants to restore our brokenness. He is waiting for us to "GO!"

Let the restoration begin.

ABOUT THE AUTHOR

Jim Ellison is married to Beth, and they have two sons, Will and Ben. He is a native of Tyrone, Georgia, a community twenty-five miles south of Atlanta.

Jim is the Executive Director of Restoration ATL, a non-profit organization in Atlanta, Georgia, that serves women and children transitioning out of homelessness. The mission creates environments of restoration through spiritual retreats that bring together persons from all walks of life.

Jim is an ordained Elder in the United Methodist Church and over the past twenty-five years, has served congregations in the Atlanta area, including the historic Atlanta First United Methodist Church.

Jim holds religious degrees from Young Harris College and LaGrange College, and a Masters of Divinity from Emory University, Atlanta, Georgia. In 2005, Jim earned a Doctorate of Ministry from Asbury Theological Seminary, Wilmore, Kentucky.

Jim enjoys thrift store shopping with his wife, fishing with his sons, and watching college football.

For more information about the author or Restoration ATL, please visit RestorationATL.org.